QUICK PREP

Surviving Litigation

What You Need to Know

Troy S. Bundy

For additional copies or customer service inquiries, please e-mail west.customer.service@thomson.com.

ISBN 978-0-314-29235-3

Mat #41670378

ACKNOWLEDGMENT

This work could not have been completed without all of the lessons learned from my colleagues, mentors, and clients throughout the years. My most special thanks to John Hart, Mark Wagner, Connie McKelvey, Steve Jones, Bob Keating, Larry Brisbee, Chuck Paulson, Mark Bocci, Larry Sokol, Jeff Wihtol, and Rich Rogers for bringing out the very best, and worst, in me as a lawyer and strategist. Of course, I also need to give a thankful nod to those little-appreciated and highly skilled claims specialists like Steve Davies, Brian Boe, Nancy Pugh, Kim Shepard, Norene Quam, Teresa Keeney, Bob Stephens, Sherry Heying, Mike Dorr, and Terrence Loeber. Without their support, many of our best ideas would not have made it off the drawing board or perhaps even been inspired.

DEDICATION

To my family for living the life demanded of a trial lawyer's family. Thank you for your unwavering support and understanding. I love you all.

CONTENTS

Introduction

If you are reading this book, the likelihood is that you are either about to be sued or have already been sued in a civil court; some of you might be potential plaintiffs. If you happen to be one of my frequent adversaries, thank you for thinking enough of me to prepare your client in advance.

Over the course of the last twenty years, I have been defending clients in civil court. There are a number of courts utilized in the civil litigation process, and I intend to touch on each one of those venues in the pages that follow.

What I would like to impart to the reader most of all is that there are not always "definite answers" to the questions that might arise during the course of a lawsuit. Additionally, this book should not be considered a substitute for person-to-person legal advice from your lawyer. As in all professional occupations, strategy choices will vary depending on the facts and circumstances in any given case. Instead, you might consider this book as a resource to educate yourself in general terms about the process, so that you can ask your own lawyer the right questions at the right time.

Further, not all state laws and courts are identical. As will be discussed in more detail, a good trial lawyer will have a sense for the court, judge, opposing counsel, and facts he or she is dealing with in protecting your interests. For those of you who have never been through the process before, it will seem like a foreign country. Some of us have even named this new world that you are about to enter: "Planet Litigation." Many of the topics and subjects will be presented as an issue involving common sense. Others may seem straightforward at first, but, after careful evaluation, your attorney's explanation may seem rather complex and even convoluted in some instances. If you have questions about strategy, the law, or any other case-specific topic, you should address those directly with the lawyer you have chosen to represent your interests.

In general, the principles that will be discussed in this book are applicable in the majority of tort law claims. Tort law can involve claims for negligence, defamation, assault, workers' compensation, sexual harassment, other employment claims, and just about every other covered specialty within the general field of personal injury law. Over the course of my career, I have represented both plaintiffs and defendants. However, the majority of my career has been defending clients. The cases I handle have ranged from automobile accidents, slips and falls, employment discrimination, defamation, sexual harassment, and professional negligence claims, to name a few.

1

Preparing for Litigation

If you have the luxury of reviewing this book prior to either being sued or filing suit, this chapter will assist you in preserving facts, details, and memories about the events that have given rise to a potential claim or lawsuit. If you have already been sued, hopefully, this chapter will help you in preparing the necessary materials you might need to preserve as much of your memory and the evidence as is possible. The key to succeeding in litigation, whether it is as a plaintiff or defendant, is in preparedness. With any luck, at the moment, you still have the ability to assist your attorney in preparing your case.

Evidence is a tool. The more tools you can provide your attorney, and the earlier you are able to provide them, the more likely your case will be either successfully prosecuted or defended on your behalf.

Before we jump into the preservation of evidence, certain key words should be defined, so there is no confusion during this discussion. A "*plaintiff*" is an individual or group of individuals who, in civil court, bring(s) a lawsuit against a *defendant* or *defendants*. A "defendant," much as it sounds, is the individual, group, or corporation that has to "defend" the lawsuit that has been brought against him, her, or it. There may be more than one defendant, in which case the defendant may have other "co-defendants." *Co-defendants* can share the same interests, but they can also be in conflict with one another about the facts and/or who is liable, if anyone.

In the event that one defendant believes another party has not been appropriately sued, that defendant can become a "*third-party plaintiff*" by bringing another party into the lawsuit. So, one can be, in any given lawsuit, a defendant as well as a third-party plaintiff. In most cases, however, there will be only one or two plaintiffs and perhaps one or two defendants. In a motor vehicle accident, for instance, there may be claims brought by one driver against another. This would result in a situation with a single plaintiff and a single defendant. However, if there were multiple drivers involved, there might be a single plaintiff, defendants, and multiple third-party defendants brought in by the originally named defendants. One can see how convoluted this might seem to someone who is unfamiliar with these terms and the law. For that reason, for purposes of the discussion in this book, there will be an assumption that we are dealing with a single plaintiff and a single defendant.

One of the most important things in representing a client in a lawsuit is to understand and prepare his or her "account," so that a jury composed of six to twelve strangers from all walks of life can understand it and apply those facts to the law in a way that is consistent with the judge's instructions at the end of trial. The easier it is for the jury to grasp the chain of events and facts leading to the claim, the more likely it will be that your attorney can effectively represent you in court.

To be a good trial lawyer, it is my firm belief that you must understand and "believe" the account your client provides. It is noteworthy, however, that sometimes those facts will negatively impact your case. Nevertheless, an attorney who is prepared and understands the truth and the facts, good and bad, will be able to more effectively represent your interests in court.

You should know that an attorney is obligated to protect your interests and to zealously advocate on your behalf no matter what. Only when lawyers are provided the complete picture can we provide the most appropriate legal advice for you during your lawsuit. That advice may not only be to go to trial, but also to try to resolve the case as quickly as possible and under reasonable terms.

In short, do not "candy-coat" the facts as you remember them. Bring out for your lawyer all relevant details that you can remember clearly. If there are gaps in your memory, and there usually are, let your attorney know this. Together, with additional facts, witness testimony, and information, it may be possible to "fill those gaps in" as the litigation progresses. If there happens to be an absolutely horrible fact, it is far better to reveal that information before the information surfaces unexpectedly through some other source. You should know, by the way, that the information always tends to surface at some point. If your lawyer has an opportunity to prepare in that regard, the impact of those negative facts will be significantly diminished. If you do not give your lawyer the benefit of the doubt, they may withdraw from the case entirely.

What follows is a detailed list of the type of information your attorney will need to either prosecute or defend your case successfully. This list is not intended to be exhaustive of all potential evidence. Instead, it will be your guide. Most attorneys have no way of knowing exactly what type of information might be available to their clients and which information might be relevant to the claims that have been brought. It is important that you not make those determinations for yourself. Even if you believe the information is not relevant, you should let your lawyer decide whether it is relevant or not. Sometimes, cases turn on the smallest detail. For instance, I have had more than one case turn on a single sentence or word contained within a patient's medical chart.

Written Statements

People often wonder whether they should write down what happened in their own words. The concern is that the documentation will be provided to your adversary. This is a very reasonable concern and, I must admit, this is often the case. However, it is my firm belief that documenting, in as much detail as possible, what occurred at the time of the events is more often than not to your own personal benefit.

Before preparing this statement or chronology of events, you should obtain a special notebook, rather than scribbling notes in haste on a napkin or scrap paper. Those items are likely to become lost during the process and may wreak havoc during the course of litigation in the event your adversary learns that you did prepare notes and have since "lost them." The argument would be that you hid or destroyed those notes intentionally in an effort to protect yourself. In that event, opposing attorneys might be able to convince a judge to read to your jury, at the time of trial, a jury instruction that directs them to "assume" that the facts and details contained within the document that was lost were unhelpful to your case and, instead, supported the other side's version of the facts. So, it is important to safeguard and maintain a written journal about the facts, if you are able to do so.

The reason I am directing you to keep a written journal is that an electronic journal might create further discovery problems down the line. Oftentimes, it is possible for computer forensic experts to access your hard drive and determine the words that were changed, sentences that were stricken, amendments that occurred later in the case versus earlier, etc. With a written record, there will be no issue concerning whether you wrote down something that you later deleted or added subsequently.

Once you have secured an appropriate journal of some type, prepare an introduction. That introduction should read: "I am preparing this document in anticipation of litigation and on the advice of counsel. The only reason for preparing these entries is so that I can provide this information to my lawyers. It represents my privileged attorney-client communication and work product."

This entry will provide you with the best protection available in preventing the opposing attorney from taking control of these notes later on in the litigation. It is definitely not foolproof, and the judge may order the documents disclosed, anyway. Nevertheless, this is probably the most you can do.

Given the foregoing, it is in your interests to assume when writing down the details that these documents will ultimately be turned over to the other side. For that reason, it is important for you to carefully consider the language you write and the words you choose to describe the events. Some of the more helpful things to write down are direct quotes from the people involved. Additionally, if you are capable of reading a "trigger word," rather than writing down a whole sentence, you should do so. Beware, however, a trigger word today may amount to nothing more than a scribble two or three years down the road, when the case is being litigated.

It might also be helpful for you to write down the details in this journal in pencil, rather than ink. Lead generally contains the same properties as it did ten or twenty years ago. Ink, on the other hand, changes all of the time. There are forensic document examiners who are capable of identifying the date a batch of ink was prepared based on a small pinprick sample of the document. Additionally, if you should realize you are mistaken about some of the details written on the paper, it is far easier to erase pencil than it is to scribble out ink. In the event you do use ink and have to "scribble out" an incorrect or poorly documented detail, you should simply rewrite the entire page and remove the page from the notebook to avoid inaccurate criticism that you were simply trying to scribble out a fact that was not favorable to your case.

In addition to the written diary that you are preparing for your lawyer, other pieces of paper or photographs might come your way. These types of documents can easily be slipped into your journal and preserved for later use.

This journal can also be used to document a number of other details that do not technically involve the facts and circumstances leading up to the lawsuit. Instead, if you have been injured, you can also use this diary to carefully detail any particular injuries you are suffering or pain you are experiencing because of the claims. You should know, however, that this portion of the journal would almost certainly be discoverable by the other side. For that reason, it might be worthwhile to start a different "pain diary" that can be provided separately for your lawyer. A pain diary can even be as simple as a calendar detailing times of appointments, pain level, important events, etc.

Other details you might want to include in your journal would be the names and addresses of eyewitnesses to events. You can identify who the individual is, what your history is with that individual, and what they saw or might have seen associated with the events in the lawsuit.

Calendars

Oftentimes, the timing of events is critical. Those events may have occurred over the course of hours or they may also have occurred over days, months, or years. Think in advance what documentation you might already have that would allow you to either recall a more detailed timeline or provide proof that those events occurred.

As recent events have shown, it is relatively easy to track an individual and their movements throughout our system today. If you went to a bank machine, there should be a record of that transaction. There may also be videotape. If you went through an intersection, there may be traffic video as well. If you saw a movie and purchased tickets online, there should be proof of that event. Telephone calls and texts could have been sent, as well as e-mails. Each of these types of electronic data is traceable and can often result in the creation of a helpful timeline. Your journal, as previously mentioned, should be updated to include this type of detail, if timing is important.

Electronic Communication

Over the course of the last decade, electronic discovery has taken on a life of its own. The meta-data contained within the electronic communication, whether it is text, e-mail, photograph, video, or otherwise, provides significant information about the underlying data. It is possible to determine when it was prepared, where it was prepared, whether it was received, whether it was changed or deleted, etc. For instance, photographs taken with a cell phone may contain meta-data that will identify the exact time and location of the photo. This is why lawyers always request a digital copy of the image, rather than a printed copy.

For this reason, great care must be taken to ensure that you have appropriately saved and disclosed to your attorney all necessary electronic forms of communication that relate to your case. It should be fairly common knowledge these days that data is never permanently destroyed. The vast majority of it can be discovered through various IT forensic work.

If there are a number of e-mails and photographs relating to your lawsuit that are contained within your various e-mail addresses, personal and otherwise, you should transfer each and every one of those documents/photographs/video to a separate sub-file within your system and be diligent about saving them in one separate file. If you are able to provide an affidavit or testimony to the court that you have exercised a diligent practice in saving all electronic data in a single sub-file, the likelihood that you will have to disgorge your complete computer system and hard drive is slight. The reality is that you need to be able to honestly tell your lawyer that you have saved everything. The judge will have to engage in a "balancing test" to determine whether the lawyer who has requested your computer hard drive has discovery rights that outweigh your own personal privacy interests.

That said, you should prepare each text and e-mail that relates to this litigation very carefully. E-mails are notoriously capable of being misinterpreted, as are text messages.

You should know that texts and e-mails are capable of being saved by your service providers for many years. Each carrier has its own rules and policy associated with the preservation of electronic documentation. AT&T, for instance, has a policy of retaining call logs and text details for five to seven years. Sprint's retention policy for this data is only two years. Therefore, it is important for you to understand that your electronic communications, deleted or not, are still available in most cases if the opposing lawyer subpoenas your service provider.

Social Networking

Social networking sites, such as Facebook, LinkedIn, and others, are commonplace. Many people have accounts. Some routinely use their account and others only look at it sporadically from time to time. You should know that, if you are a party to a lawsuit, both your lawyer and the opposing lawyer will attempt to review your publicly available information. Your lawyer does this to protect you from yourself. The opposing attorney will do this to look for "bad facts." If you do utilize one of these networks, it is not in your interests to post details about the claim or lawsuit in which you are involved. Many people often seek moral support from “friends” on these networks. You should assume that this information is subject to discovery and will be requested by the opposing attorney. In some instances, the opposing attorney will subpoena the service provider and obtain a string of posts associated with the lawsuit and other personal details about your life. Facebook’s own website contains a detailed procedure that instructs lawyers how to obtain post information on its users. They are obligated to provide it when properly subpoenaed.

If you wish to keep one of these social network sites open, and most attorneys would tell their clients not to do so, please make sure it is capable of the imposition of certain “privacy protections.” In other words, if any stranger can review your profile or network information without being accepted as a “friend,” you should review the service provider’s site instructions or contact them to make changes to your account, such that it is privileged and private.

Also, although most of us believe it would be unethical to surreptitiously access a private network account to investigate a claim by using fraudulent techniques, there are those who believe that third parties may do so and then provide the information to the lawyer. There are not a great number of detailed ethics opinions covering this topic. Nevertheless, I take the position that any third party acting on my interests is, in fact, acting as my agent. An agent cannot do anything that I, as a lawyer, cannot do. So, misleading someone into believing that the third party is a “friend” would be unethical in every jurisdiction I am aware of.

That said, some attorneys also believe there is a “gray area” when it comes to this type of interaction. For instance, what if a third person simply sends a “friend request,” but does not “mislead” the individual at all? Some people simply “accept” any kind of “invitation” from a potential contact and allow them into their private network. In other words, choose your “friends” carefully.

Finally, it will be important for you to disassociate yourself with any social club memberships that might be deemed inappropriate. If you believe you would find yourself feeling embarrassed by belonging to certain "social network clubs," you should unsubscribe from those clubs immediately. For instance, I once defended a nurse in a malpractice case who belonged to a "professional" social media club titled: *"I'm Your Nurse, Not Your F'ing Maid!"* Of course, although it might seem as though this "tongue in cheek" group was somewhat funny to professional nurses, your average patient or juror would not find this funny at all and I, as your lawyer, would be spending considerable time attempting to prevent the plaintiff's attorney from asking you questions about that group while you are on the witness stand in court. A good rule of thumb is to simply avoid participating in groups that would be poorly received by the general public. You must assume that any information you can uncover about yourself by conducting a general name search, together with a few key words, would be discovered by the opposing party and their lawyer. Do not embarrass yourself and do not jeopardize your own case or liability exposure by sustaining memberships in "off color" social media groups.

Photographs

One of the most insidious adversaries any attorney can face is time. As the saying goes, time waits for no one. It destroys memories and understanding. Scenes, equipment, property damage, and injuries change over time. The other saying that is absolutely true is that "a picture is worth a thousand words." As time changes the details of your case, it might also destroy the strength of your arguments or diminish the value of your injuries.

Take the Trayvon Martin case, for example. What was more effective: explaining to the jury that the George Zimmerman suffered a broken nose and scalp injuries or, rather, the photos that illustrated his misshapen bridge and blood-covered head? The jury answered that question.

The lesson is to take photos or video of everything that might be of importance later. Injuries, healing or infected wounds, property damage, accident scenes, the lack of injuries on your own body, equipment at issue, posted traffic signs, or any other detail you can think of that is associated with your case. Most lawyers sit behind a desk and review documents. Any bit of information that might help them tell your story will be important.

If you are using a digital camera to record evidence, make sure you are utilizing a high-resolution setting on the camera/phone. Poor resolution/grainy photographs are virtually worthless in court.

Autopsy

If you are unfortunate enough to be considering a wrongful death lawsuit, you must decide whether an autopsy is in order. Some autopsies are State-mandated. Deaths involving children, for instance, generally require autopsy. Deaths under mysterious or unexplained circumstances, including homicide, are also subject to the mandatory autopsy rules.

You should discuss these details with the "attending physician," assuming one has been assigned to the deceased. If there is not an attending physician, ask to speak with "risk management" in the hospital about the possibilities for autopsy. Most of the time, it is done at the request of the deceased's family. If the hospital does not or will not perform the autopsy, it may be necessary to retain a forensic pathologist to perform an independent study.

You should consider retaining a lawyer who is experienced in handling wrongful death cases. Any good plaintiff's injury attorney will know the names of local, independent forensic pathologists. Typically, they are retired county coroners who are still licensed to perform this type of dissection.

Whatever the case, insist on photographic documentation of the procedure. This is vital evidence that can be utilized for many facets of the case, and may increase the likelihood that your pathologist's testimony will be both admissible in court and harder for the opposing attorney to "rebut."

Receipts

To recover for "economic damages," a plaintiff must prove the loss. Receipts, canceled checks, bills, and other evidence of payments must be saved and presented into evidence. Oral testimony is not convincing. Most of the time, opposing counsel will simply "stipulate" or agree at trial that the documentation sufficiently establishes a specific amount of economic loss. Without documentation of actual loss, most defense lawyers will deny the loss exists, and the alleged loss will not be awarded.

911 Calls

If you have been involved in an accident or if an ambulance or emergency medical personnel were summoned on the telephone for whatever reason, you must work quickly to obtain a copy of the emergency call telephone conversation. Each and every one of those telephone calls is recorded. However, those recordings are routinely destroyed after a relatively short period. Typically, you have ninety to 120 days to request a copy of the actual audio recording.

These recordings have come in very handy when dealing with cases involving traumatic injuries, suicides, and other unexpected deaths or injuries.

Handouts, Books, and Pamphlets

In medical cases, many patients receive various pamphlets and handouts from their physicians' offices. Sometimes these handouts are simply available in the waiting room and are located on shelves or tables. On occasion, patients are given a bag full of information relating to various topics, such as surgeries they might be undergoing, intensive medical treatments they may be preparing for, or even prenatal care bags full of information. These documents should be preserved.

It is difficult at times to obtain the actual materials that were either given to or available to the patient at the time care was rendered. Years can pass and materials can be lost or changed over the course of time. It is important to know what was reviewed by the patient and what was, perhaps, capable of being reviewed by the patient at the time. This instruction would go both ways to either a physician or a patient who is involved in litigation.

As far as books or booklets are concerned, to the extent they relate to the case, they should also be preserved. Whether it is an employee handbook, policy manual, book of regulations, or any number of other documents, if they relate to the tort case, it will save your attorney a significant amount of time tracking these things down if you have them at the ready.

Medical Records

Every person who is a patient in the United States has access to his or her complete medical record. If emergency room care was rendered, a copy of the emergency room chart should be obtained. The same goes for any care provided in an ambulance, by the fire department, by a medical clinic, hospital, or other medical provider. Obtaining a complete copy of your medical chart directly from the service provider will save you and your attorney a great deal of time and expense.

When, and if, the medical records are turned over to your attorney, they should not be "cherry picked" for the best, most supportive records. Instead, a complete copy should be provided to your lawyer to ensure the best proper legal analysis.

To obtain your records, you should contact your service provider's "records custodian." Simply place a telephone call and speak with the records custodian, inquiring what documentation they will need to release a complete copy of your medical chart. Depending on the volume of materials contained within that chart, it could take up to fourteen days to obtain a complete copy.

When requesting a copy of your chart, make sure you ask for every possible document contained within the record. Since many hospitals and clinics use an "electronic medical record," production of a medical chart is not as easy as it used to be. A request should be made for all documents including all notes, orders, e-mails, memoranda, labs, radiology reports, radiographs, letters, referrals, orders, prescriptions, attendance logs, progress notes, reports of all kinds, insurance communications, billing summaries, patient handouts, anesthesia records, medical administration record, flow sheets, and any other document of any kind, sort, or nature included within the patient's record. Even then, you should be prepared for the fact that the records custodian may still have not provided you with your entire medical file. It all depends, honestly, on the scope of experience the records custodian has in responding to this type of request. Custodians are notoriously unreliable in this respect.

Texts and Journals

Inevitably, in a professional negligence case, the defendants will be asked to produce a list or the title page of all texts and periodicals they own relating to the allegations in the lawsuit. Whether you are a lawyer, physician, architect, engineer or some other professional, you probably have a library filled with outdated materials. In fact, I would not be surprised if you have not accessed most of those materials in many years.

The reality is that many lawyers would argue you are responsible for knowing what every single one of those textbooks says. If you do not, and you fail to follow the guidelines, rules, or recommendations set out in those texts, this would be evidence that you violated what is known as the "standard of care." The standard of care, in the legal context, is that standard by which most reasonable and careful professionals in your specialty, in your community, would do under the same or similar circumstances at the time the services were rendered.

If you have not been sued, my suggestion would be that you review your library and dispose of any old, outdated texts or journals that you do not reference. There is no sense in keeping these documents, as they will only create a hassle for you in the event a lawsuit arises sometime in the future. A professional's library, especially a professional who is at risk for becoming involved in litigation, should be limited specifically to those texts and journals the professional relies on and uses on a regular basis. Otherwise, they simply take up space and have the potential of being used against you in a lawsuit sometime down the road.

If you are already involved in a lawsuit, you should not take this advice as inferring or instructing you to destroy evidence. To the contrary, my suggestion at that point would be to ensure that you do not destroy any documentation of any kind whatsoever for fear of being sanctioned or turning an innocuous, perhaps even helpful, journal or text into a nail in your coffin. This advice is intended to be only a proactive recommendation.

In the event you are sued and a request for production is tendered by the opposing attorney, they will in all likelihood ask for this type of material. If you have to disclose the fact that you destroyed the evidence after you were sued, the opposing attorney would have a very good argument that you should be held in contempt or for sanctions and/or that you should also be subject to the "spoliation of evidence" instructions. Do not underestimate a lawyer's ability to discover what the state of evidence was at the time the lawsuit was initiated. Destroying evidence is the fastest way to destroy an otherwise meritorious case.

Answering Machine Recordings

In the event there are audio recordings on an answering machine or voicemail of some sort, you should make every effort to preserve those recordings. Even if it is necessary to make an audio recording of an audio recording using two different devices, you should do that. Never destroy a voicemail that relates to the case. Additionally, I would strongly encourage you not to leave your own voicemail in another individual's mailbox when you are involved in potential litigation. Any voicemail you leave on a witness's recorder should be assumed by you to be in the possession of the opposing attorney. The best strategy is to simply call the person back and speak directly with them.

Phone Tapping

You should know that, in some states, it is legal to tape record a private telephone call between you and someone else without disclosing the fact that the conversation is being recorded. In Oregon, for instance, a party need only have the "consent of one." In other words, if I am carrying on a private telephone conversation with anyone at all, I can tape record that conversation without telling the other person on the line. If you feel as though you are being tape recorded, you should inquire of the individual on the other end of the line whether that is, in fact, happening. They may lie to you. However, at least you will have created an issue as to their credibility in the event a damaging telephone call recording comes up in the course of discovery.

However, in every state of the union, it is absolutely illegal to record that same conversation if the conversation is in person. If the individual is unaware that the conversation is being recorded, and the communication is occurring on a person-to-person basis, it requires a warrant. As such, the party who is illicitly recorded can not only demand that the tape be excluded from evidence, but they can also ask the district attorney to institute a criminal proceeding against the person making the recording without consent.

For the above reasons, be extremely careful if you decide to tape record an individual surreptitiously after an incident that gave rise to a legal claim. My suggestion is that it is best left to your lawyer. Further, in the event there is some unusual opportunity to obtain helpful statements from your opponent or eyewitnesses in the case, you will have to determine for yourself whether the law allows such a taping and whether or not the taping would be at all helpful to you sometime down the road. One of the examples of this that comes to mind are the Mel Gibson tapes, which were recorded by his ex-girlfriend, Oksana Grigorieva, and used in their custody proceedings involving their eight-month-old daughter. If you have not heard the tapes, you might consider listening to how damaging recorded statements can be.

Recorded Statements

Oftentimes, an insured is asked to provide a telephonic recorded statement. The individual requesting the interview is generally an insurance claims adjuster who has been notified that a claim has been filed. The immediate question often arises concerning whether such a statement is subject to discovery and admissible in later court proceedings. The short answer is, generally, yes.

The decision to provide a recorded statement to either your own or the other individual's insurance carrier should be thoroughly considered. Of course, the majority of claims made against insurance companies are covered by the company and provide a fast way to obtain reimbursement for injuries or property damage. Additionally, if you are being asked to provide a statement by your own insurance carrier, a cooperation clause is generally contained within your insurance contract that requires your cooperation and, in most cases, a formal statement about the facts giving rise to any potential claim will be required.

In the event your own insurance carrier is asking for your statement, my general response would be to cooperate with your carrier as much as possible. However, do not give a recorded statement without being appropriately prepared. It is recommended that you think long and hard about your statement and analyze the facts, moment by moment, before giving an unprepared statement about what happened during the incident or incidents in question. Oftentimes, insurance carriers place phone calls to their insureds, and the call is not expected. An abbreviated, "off the cuff" recorded statement about the events leading up to the claim is given. It is based on this statement that your insurance carrier or the other individual's carrier will make coverage determinations. In other words, they are attempting to determine whether an insurance policy exclusion applies.

Therefore, it is advisable for you to review your insurance contract. If you are confused about the terms of the contract, you should consult with either your agent or a lawyer to help you identify coverage issues. You should know that your insurance carrier is not necessarily "your friend." Many carriers, though not all, look for ways to avoid coverage in whatever shape or form. If you are familiar with your own policy and the coverage it provides, this will help you better understand the questions they are asking, and the reasons they are asking those questions in the first place. Before affirming the "facts" of your claim, it is advisable for the insured to determine for themselves whether the claim is likely covered by their insurance. If it is not, the reasons for lack of coverage should also be considered.

The next consideration in answering this question relates to whether a lawsuit is likely. If you know that you intend to file a claim, and you are the injured party, it is advisable to secure a lawyer before giving such a statement. That attorney can appropriately advise you whether or not you should participate in the interview process, whether it is required, and the issues that might be raised. In some instances, a written statement can be submitted to the insurance carrier in lieu of a formal "interview." In such cases, plaintiffs' lawyers often prefer to prepare the statement in writing on their client's behalf.

If you are the one who is likely to be sued, most insurance contracts provide their insureds with a civil defense attorney. Insurers contract with a number of different law firms in any given region. Insurance defense attorneys, as we are called, are generally specialists in handling the types of claims that arise under insurance contracts. Those claims can include anything from an automobile accident to professional negligence to an employment discrimination claim. If there is a policy of insurance covering those potential claims, then there are law firms out there who specialize in defending claims of that nature on behalf of insurance companies and their insureds.

Since this book is geared toward individuals who are either concerned about or actively engaged in litigation, providing a recorded statement without the presence of your lawyer to an insurance company agent is something that you should be very careful about. If you have any concerns at all, the issue should be discussed with a lawyer. Many attorneys will meet with you free of charge for an hour to discuss your rights and obligations when it comes to a claim that is insured.

Physical Objects

In the event that a potential claim involves a piece of machinery or equipment, great care should be taken to preserve that evidence in the state that it was at the time of the event. Sometimes, this is simply not possible. If the equipment or other item cannot be preserved in a safe place without tampering, great care should be taken to photograph and videotape every possible detail associated with the equipment at issue. Whether it is a piece of farm machinery, an automobile or surgical stapler, visual aids are critical in either defending or prosecuting an injury claim.

In addition to photographs and videotape, all equipment manuals and diagrams should be retained, to the extent they exist. Serial numbers should be recorded as well as any other identifying marks or numbers. This would include “inspected by” tags or registrations.

Some equipment requires calibration on a regular basis. To the extent that there are calibration and service logs, those should be preserved as well. Details associated with the names or location of any service provider who performed regular inspections on the equipment or machinery should also be preserved. Do not wait for an attorney to ask you for this information.

Summary

Many pieces of evidence might either make or break any given lawsuit. Not only is it important for this information to be collected and saved, it is also important for you to provide all of this information to your lawyer without him or her having to ask you for it directly. This will avoid a piecemeal approach to discovery production, which can result in an incorrect analysis and, in rare cases, sanctions against the lawyer or the party for failing to produce these documents earlier or allowing them to be destroyed. Most clients do not realize that their attorney may be relying on the client’s expertise in dealing with the issues at hand. Not all lawyers understand exactly what is available to either prove or disprove a legal theory in the case. With the client’s assistance and full disclosure of all available documentation and other evidence, the lawyer and his or her client stand a better chance of achieving the best possible outcome at the conclusion of litigation, be it trial or otherwise.

2

Representation

As discussed in Chapter 1, many lawsuits are covered by insurance. In those cases, a potential defendant should look to all available policies of insurance that might cover the claim in question. Those can include anything from an automobile policy, professional liability policy, or homeowner's insurance. Many individuals also have umbrella policies that will cover other potential claims where the underlying policies fall short. Business owners may have general liability coverage and/or error/omission policies. It is advisable to meet with your insurance agent or broker in an effort to determine the types of insurance that you have available and whether an underlying carrier might cover a claim.

Selecting a Lawyer

Frequently, I am asked to recommend a lawyer to friends or former clients. Selecting a lawyer is a very important part of the legal process. Lawyers, just like any other profession, have certain specialties in which they practice. There are attorneys who specialize in virtually every conceivable aspect of tort law. This happened for a reason. Not every tort law is the same. Products liability cases are similar to, but not identical to negligence cases. Products liability cases may also involve general negligence cases against an owner or operator. There are toxic tort attorneys, admiralty claims specialists, workers' compensation lawyers, and the like. Over the course of time, my practice has evolved into one specializing in professional liability and health law. However, I have handled claims for many years involving various types of general liability torts including the great majority of tort claims out there.

If you happen to be a defendant, most likely your insurance carrier will assign a lawyer to handle the course and scope of your representation. That lawyer will want to meet with you and discuss the case in detail. He or she will also want all of the paperwork and other evidence described in Chapter 1.

It is important for you to know that, even though this lawyer has been assigned to you by the carrier, you do not have to accept that lawyer as your representative. You can request that the carrier appoint someone else. You can also request that the carrier appoint someone by name. Although it is fairly uncommon, the insured generally will have a say in who represents their interests. Obviously, the more complex and valuable the claim, the more a defendant should think hard and long about whom they want representing their interests at trial.

It is also not uncommon for the "prayer" contained with a complaint to exceed the value of insurance available. The "prayer" is contained in the last paragraph of a plaintiff's complaint that is filed in court. In essence, it is a demand for money.

In the event that the prayer exceeds the value of available insurance, the insurance carrier will then write the defendant a letter, known as an "excess letter," which will inform the insured of the fact that they do not have enough insurance to cover the prayer or proposed damages contained within a claim or complaint. This letter will also contain a "reservation of rights." In other words, the insurance company's duty to defend you in litigation and their duty to pay for any liability you incur are separate. Even though you may not be fully insured to cover a loss, most policies will require the insurance company to defend you 100 percent, regardless of how much is charged by the lawyer representing your interests. There are separate companies that haggle with the law firm billing services, but that is not the insured's problem to deal with.

An excess letter or letter explaining a reservation of rights will also contain language to the effect that the insured should consult with their own personal lawyer in an effort to explain their rights and liabilities associated with the contract. When this happens, defendants panic.

However, the best thing to do is to take a deep breath and schedule an appointment with your assigned lawyer to discuss your case in detail. That lawyer has an obligation to stay away from discussing any coverage issues. However, your attorney is obligated to discuss with you their analysis of the claims and the likely true exposure you might face.

As far as complaints are concerned and prayers within those complaints, there are no rules specifically stating what a lawyer must claim as damages to file a piece of paper titled "complaint" or "action at law." Most of the time, these numbers are completely unrealistic. They represent an absolute cap on the amount a party can obtain at trial. For that reason, lawyers usually overestimate the value of their case, so they do not malpractice by closing the door to additional damages their client might have recovered in the event of a run-away jury or some other case development.

An insurance defense lawyer is forbidden from acting in interests that run contrary to either the insurance company's or the insured's interests. Your lawyer should be able to explain how they "valued" your case under the circumstances. This valuation is based on experience and many other details that will be discussed in the pages that follow. For instance, the county in which the claim is seated might have an impact on damages. Additionally, the experience or skill of the opposing lawyer also plays a role in determining case value. Each of these things should be included in the lawyer's initial evaluation of the case. From there, you can determine whether it is advisable for you to retain your own lawyer and pay money out of pocket in the form of an expensive retainer.

Questions you might ask your defense lawyer include: How many years of experience they have, what their specialty is, how many cases they try every year, how many claims they handle at any given time, their success rate, their experience with the opposing attorney, etc. You should get a feel for your lawyer and determine whether you are comfortable with their representation. If you distrust your lawyer, then you should probably retain someone else.

Plaintiffs

People considering filing a lawsuit should be selective in the attorneys they consider. Many of the factors discussed above apply. The best way to find a good lawyer is to search for specialists online who have appropriate credentials. The number of years in practice is important, as well as their results.

Some companies, like Thomson Reuters, provide consumers with special guides that are worthy of mention. Super Lawyers is one of those publications. Individuals are selected for that type of award based on peer input. Consideration should be given, when researching possible attorneys, of any awards of achievements they have received. There are other rating agencies that bear mention, including The Best Lawyers in America and Martindale Hubbell publications.

Once you identify candidates, you should perform a more in-depth analysis of their skill. For instance, have they taken any time out of their day to actually design a website? On their website, have they discussed their credentials and qualifications? Are they working in a rundown warehouse underneath a bridge on the north side? Do they share space in a laundromat? These are all important questions you should ask in making your selection.

Attorney selection in any given case is important. There are lawyers within the plaintiff's bar who are respected for the work they do and, as a result, defense lawyers may even increase a damage evaluation based upon the plaintiff's lawyer's skill. There are, of course, many plaintiffs' lawyers who are personally disliked by members of the defense bar. However, their skill and ability is respected. Regardless of their "likeability," many successful plaintiffs' lawyers are known and appreciated for their tenacity and ability.

On the other hand, there are also a significant number of plaintiffs' attorneys out there who are both well liked and respected. Cases might settle for more simply because there is a mutual respect between the plaintiff's lawyer and the insurance carrier or the defense lawyer handling the claim. This respect, however, also arises from skill and ability. In essence, if you can get a defense lawyer to like you, we must assume that the jury will also agree. A likeable party/attorney is something to be wary of, if you happen to be on the opposing side.

In summary, do your research. If you happen to read about a lawsuit in the paper that was settled and it involves facts similar to yours, there is nothing preventing you from speaking with that represented party and asking them how their lawyer performed. Friends, neighbors, and relatives should also be utilized as sources of information about who to hire and who "did a great job" on their behalf. If you have been represented before by a lawyer who specializes in another area of the law, inquire of that lawyer whom they would recommend or whether there is someone they can speak with. As attorneys, we all went to law school, and we all pay attention to who is known "about town" when it comes to certain areas of the law. Sometimes, I have to direct my former clients to other lawyers, who happen to be friends of mine, to provide more detailed information or reviews of lawyers specializing in those areas.

Great care should be taken when selecting a lawyer to choose the lawyer who is right for you. In the event the lawyer is charging a fee for a one-hour consultation to discuss your plaintiff's injury case, this is probably a warning sign. Most lawyers who have a strong, active practice do not charge potential clients a consultation fee to discuss their case. Attorneys who are "worth their salt," will already have a strong client base and not need to squeeze a few hundred dollars out of potential new clients.

You should consider meeting with more than one prospective attorney. Each attorney, as will be discussed later, has a different style. Some may work with your personality and some may not. You may need a more aggressive attorney, or you might need a "kinder and gentler" approach. Not everyone gets along, but it is important that you move forward in litigation with someone you respect and trust. Litigation is a long road, and you should understand that you would be interacting with this individual for many months, or perhaps even years, to come. Choose wisely.

Scope of Representation

You should understand that information you discuss with your lawyer or potential lawyer is considered privileged. This means that the information cannot be disclosed with anyone outside of your lawyer's office. Secretaries and paralegals who work with the lawyer will be privy to this information to the extent it is contained in any of the lawyer's memorandums or notes.

However, whatever you discuss with that lawyer will remain a secret unless you give the lawyer authority to disclose the information at some later point. This is known as the attorney-client privilege.

You might also want to know that privileges are generally shared. There is a husband-wife privilege that allows husbands and wives to speak with one another during the course of their marriage and have those discussions protected. This is thought to encourage the longevity of a healthy marriage, since neither spouse can be compelled to testify against the other. Each spouse holds the privilege and can prevent the other spouse from testifying about what was discussed in most situations. Of course, exceptions to this rule exist in cases involving domestic disputes or custody issues. Other exceptions may, likewise, apply.

The most important part of this shared privilege rule is that a husband can talk to his wife about what he and his lawyer discussed without waiving any privilege. However, if the client discusses that information with anyone else, the privilege may be considered waived. This might also include discussions that the represented party has with their physician. By the way, a marital privilege does not apply to any "significant other" or "life partner" exchanges.

One might ask, "What about the physician-patient privilege?" The answer to that question is that the physician-patient privilege will only cover communications between a patient and the physician to the extent that the information relates to the care and treatment of the patient. If it is unrelated to care and treatment, conversations that were otherwise privileged will be discoverable by the opposing side. There have been a number of occasions that have arisen during my practice where confidential attorney-client information is shared by a plaintiff patient to their medical provider. That medical provider, in turn, mentions something in passing in the written medical chart. Once I receive the medical chart, I will be able to argue that the attorney-client privilege in that context has been permanently waived by the claimant. .

So, although an attorney-client privilege does exist, it is important to understand that the information exchanged is still vulnerable to discovery, if it is not handled appropriately. The only two people an individual should be discussing attorney-client conversations with are their wife/husband or priest.

3

Litigation Expense

Personal Expenses and Costs

Litigation is not cheap. There are many costs of litigation associated with both bringing and defending a claim. Oftentimes, represented parties have a misunderstanding of exactly what is covered and not covered by the attorney's fee agreement.

If you happen to be defended by an insurance carrier and an appointed lawyer, you should not be billed or have to pay any out-of-pocket costs associated with the litigation. If you happen to be in an excess situation, as discussed in Chapter 1, you may have to pay fees or costs associated with that individual. However, for the most part, all fees and expenses are covered by your carrier.

In the event that you are considering bringing a claim, most tort lawyers work based on what is known as a contingency fee agreement. This agreement is generally governed by your local state bar's rules of ethics. Some state bars have a form contingency fee agreement; most do not.

In very general terms, a percentage of any recovery will be considered the "attorney's fee" your lawyer will collect. Depending on how your lawyer has drawn this up, it should generally involve a different percentage depending on the stage at which your claim resolves. For instance, if the claim is settled before it is filed, your attorney may require a 25 percent contingency fee. If the matter is filed, but is settled before trial, the fee agreement might require payment of 33.3 percent. In the event the case goes to trial, your lawyer may be entitled to 40 percent, and so on. I have seen contingency fee agreements that go up through the appeals process and might ultimately result in an attorney's fee recovery in the 50 to 60 percent range.

The rules of professional ethics prohibit attorneys from agreeing to cover fees and costs associated with the litigation. To do so would, in the state bar association's eyes, result in the attorney obtaining a "stake in the litigation." This is prohibited, supposedly. That said, I think we are all aware of the fact that contingent fee lawyers always have a "stake in the litigation."

For the above-stated reason, the fee agreements typically contain a cost and expense section that states the client will be responsible for paying all costs and expenses associated with the claim. Costs and expenses will include filing fees, deposition fees, court reporter's fees, copy expenses, service fees, expert witness fees, jury fees, motion fees, etc. In short, the court system has developed a number of ways to collect money from litigants to pay its bills. The cost of filing fees continues to rise as courts are deprived of appropriate budget funding. Some courts have gone so far as to charge more for filing for claims in which the prayer exceeds a certain amount. For instance, one particular county I am aware of charges more for the filing of claims involving a prayer exceeding $1 million and also charges more for filing a claim involving multiple defendants. There is, essentially, no end to the amount of fees and costs associated with litigation and trial.

When it comes to calculating the amounts recoverable at the end of a case, many contingency fee agreements will provide that the lawyer gets their "cut" first. Then, costs and expenses are subtracted from the client's portion of the recovery. I have also seen some contingency fee agreements that subtract costs first and then split the balance in accordance with the percentage allocated to the attorney and client per contract. This can result in a significant difference in a plaintiff's recovery.

As an example, assume there is a settlement at trial for $100,000. The costs and expenses of bringing that case to trial amount to $25,000 between all of the experts, exhibits, and discovery work that has gone into the case. If we were to apply the former distribution of proceeds, the lawyer would recover

$40,000 in fees, $25,000 would then be reimbursed to the lawyer to cover costs and expenses, and this would leave $35,000 for the client (assuming we are working with a 40 percent contingency at trial). If we were to apply the latter format, $25,000 would be taken from the top to cover costs and expenses. This would leave $75,000 to be distributed between the attorney and client. With a 40 percent fee agreement in place, the plaintiff's lawyer would recover $30,000, resulting in a $45,000 payment to the plaintiff. In other words, it is all in the math.

Time

Lawsuits take a great deal of time to prepare. You should be aware of the fact that your attorney will be asking you for a great deal of documentation including what was discussed in Chapter 1. Inevitably, other particulars of your case will necessitate your personal involvement. It is important for you to discuss with your lawyer the amount of involvement expected of you. Some cases involve a great deal of work on the part of the represented party, others do not. For the most part, the client's role is relegated to collecting the necessary discovery requested by the opposing attorney, appearing for a deposition, preparing for trial, and attending trial.

Lost time from work cannot be underestimated. This time spent preparing for litigation is not a recoverable part of your claim. If you are scheduled for trial for two weeks, you are not entitled to reimbursement of your time regardless of whether you win at trial or not. This is a cost of litigation and not a cost of the actual claim.

Reviewing your library, garage, file room or whatever for the requested discovery will take time. It is imperative that you take the necessary time to get this done. In the event additional discovery surfaces at some point during the course of litigation because you have not taken the time to engage in a meaningful search for the documents requested, you will face potential sanctions including money damages or even a dismissal of your claim or defenses. In essence, whether you are a plaintiff or defendant, you should take a substantial amount of time to confirm what documents you have or do not have when it comes to discovery requests.

In addition to engaging in discovery work, the keeping of a journal or other notes as requested by your lawyer will also be in order. The better you are at doing this, and the more time you take to be actively involved in your lawsuit, the more likely it is that your litigation will be successful.

Depositions are also part of the discovery process. As will be discussed in more detail later, a deposition merely provides an opportunity for the opposing lawyer to interview you and obtain your statement and account under oath. Depending on the complexity of your case, significant time might be spent preparing you for your deposition. It might take a matter of hours, or it could take a matter of days. Much depends on whether your lawyer believes you are "presenting" as a witness in the best possible light. If you already "present well," you will probably need less time to prepare. If you are nervous and stammering, your lawyer will want to take additional time to make sure you are comfortable providing testimony in front of the opposing lawyer.

Pretrial preparation is also important. Many lawyers will take time with their clients before a trial occurs to prepare them for what lies ahead. Trials can take days or months to complete. In my practice, most trials last approximately two weeks. Others might involve a four-day trial or even a month-long trial. Your lawyer will be able to give you a better idea of how long you can expect to be out of work. As mentioned above, keep in mind, your lost income will not be reimbursed as an expense of trial. Some insurance contracts, however, do provide a daily "stipend" for every day spent in court, if you are operating under a professional liability policy.

It will be important for you to note trial dates on your calendar as early as possible. This should enable you to plan accordingly by saving vacation days or working extra hours in the months before and after a trial occurs. Always try to get a sense from your lawyer how long he or she expects to take to try the case. Oftentimes, your lawyer will be unable to answer this question because it is unclear how long the opposing side will take during their case.

In civil court, there is a considerable amount of time spent arguing pretrial motions and selecting a jury. Jury selection is known as "*voir dire*." The process can take anywhere from several hours to several days. The facts of the case and the media exposure the case has generated will generally dictate how long it takes to select a jury. There are also opening statements, presentation of the plaintiff's case-in-chief, the presentation of defendant's case-in-chief, the plaintiff's presentation of rebuttal witnesses, final arguments before the court, and jury instructions. From there, the jury will move on to deliberations, and this will take "however long it takes." Civil trials that last two or three days are few and far between.

The message here is to plan ahead. Communicate with your lawyer about timing and the scope of your involvement. Litigation involves a tremendous amount of work. Your lawyer will do the lion's share, but your lack of involvement in litigation is usually not an option.

Liens

It is also worth noting that there may be a number of medical liens or other liens out there that require consideration. In the event the claimant has been injured and treated, the cost of that treatment will become part of the prayer or demand made by the plaintiff. There may be a notice of lien filed by the plaintiff's insurance carrier or by any other number of organizations including emergency personnel, property damage insurers, physical therapists, emergency room care, surgical care, radiology, pharmacy, and any other number of companies out there that have paid money for services or goods as a result of the accident or claim in question. This even includes the workers' compensation division in your state, to the extent it was involved.

If we are talking about medical liens, there are three evaluations to be considered. Any good defense lawyer knows that the amount billed for any health care service will not be the amount ultimately paid by the plaintiff, if the claim is settled. In the first place, not all amounts billed are actually paid by insurance. Insurance companies have separate agreements with individual care providers setting out the maximum amounts they can charge for covered services. Typically, the amount covered is substantially less than the amount billed.

So, in a situation where the insurance carrier has paid $80,000 on a $100,000 bill, the insurance carrier will have a lien in the amount of $80,000 against any potential defendant. The balance in most cases is generally written off by the care provider for tax purposes. In the event that the hospital seeks reimbursement from the patient, that amount would be considered an out-of-pocket loss to the plaintiff and is recoverable. However, keeping this discussion limited to liens, as a general rule of thumb, one can expect a one-third reduction in any lien amount at the end of the day. Insurance carriers understand that recovery is not guaranteed and they will essentially "settle" on the lien they hold in your case. A good plaintiffs' lawyer will be able to give you some idea of the actual amounts an insurance carrier will write off.

Although these details cannot be confirmed with any degree of certainty, when I see medical bills in the amount of $100,000, and I know there is a medical lien in the amount of $80,000, I assume that the plaintiff will probably be able to settle with the carrier for between $50,000 to 60,000.

Again, the ability to settle with the carrier will depend significantly upon your attorney's abilities, their relationship and past experience with the carrier, and the amount of leverage they actually have at the time the lien is negotiated. Your lawyer may try to create leverage in settling your case by explaining to the carrier how unlikely it is you would recover in the event of a trial. He or she might also discuss unhelpful or damaging facts in your case, and it may seem like your lawyer is "against you." Nevertheless, they are simply doing their job by attempting to maximize your recovery.

That said, most contingency fee agreements would include lien costs as an expense. By law, liens must be resolved first before monies are paid to you or the lawyer.

If Medicare or Medicaid is involved, this will create a significant problem for all attorneys involved. Federal agencies are notoriously difficult to deal with. The amount of red tape involved and their seeming lack of interest in achieving a productive result for all involved is woefully inadequate.

If you happen to be unfortunate enough to have a Medicare or Medicaid lien, be prepared for the fact that your case will take extra time to deal with and settle. There are also "future care and treatment" costs that have to be considered when dealing with Medicare and Medicaid. Lawyers and insurers have personal liability exposure to the government, if the lien is not handled correctly or consistently with the rules and regulations affecting those liens.

Emotional Toll

Lawsuits drag on. It is the nature of the beast who is held captive in an underfunded governmental structure that must provide a "speedy trial" to those charged with crimes. The result can be a delayed civil process. Different jurisdictions will have different "time to trial" dockets. Your case may take six months to be resolved or it may take six years to be resolved. The amount of damages, parties involved, complexity of claims, amount of discovery required, type of claims, and expected length of trial all come to bear in determining where your case will fall on the "bell curve" when it comes to a speedy case resolution.

A lawsuit is something in the back of your mind whether you are a plaintiff or a defendant. Personal injury cases involve emotionally charged issues. They can also have career and other professional implications. As a result, they have a tendency to sap your emotional strength and stability. That said, your lawyer is not a substitute for a mental health professional. Depression and self-doubt is commonplace. Deal with these issues as they arise. Consider counseling and medications, if the litigation "takes over." People handle stress in different ways. But, regardless, be prepared to recognize that litigation, depending on its form, may affect your personal relationships and professional life. If others start to notice, you need to raise these matters with your regular care provider. Some lawyers can also refer you to specialized litigation counselors in your area.

Do not let the litigation "take" any more from you than either your injury or the claims against you already have. Some of my clients prefer a "need to know" communication, others request to be more involved. Let your lawyer know how they can help you handle the mental costs. Sometimes, it is as simple as changing the form or extent of ongoing communications between you and your lawyer.

4

The Courthouse Steps

The document filed with the court must contain a number of details relating to the claim at issue. Some states require no more than a general complaint that someone did something "negligent." Other states require the individual filing the complaint to name a number of "particulars" in which they believe the defendant was negligent or committed a tort. The word "tort" does not refer to a dessert. It embodies any number of causes of action that give rise to civil liability. A car accident, defamation, discrimination, assault and battery, professional mistake, fraud, etc., are all "torts."

Once a lawyer representing the plaintiff files this document, called a complaint, they must "serve" the complaint on the named defendant. Many people think they can avoid service of process by simply not answering the doorbell when it rings. This is wrong and will ultimately prove to be a grave mistake. When served with a complaint, usually by a process server or local sheriff, the defendant should simply accept the service and notify the appropriate insurance carriers. Contrary to popular belief, ditching a process server does you no good. In fact, it may increase your liability and exposure.

As an aside, the term "exposure" refers to the likelihood that a defendant could be required to pay money to someone else. The more "exposure" you have, the more likely it is that a defendant will be found liable for damages. The term "exposure" means just that. In other words, the more "exposure" you have, the more "naked" you are to being found responsible for harm to another person. You have less "protection" from the claim.

The reason I would suggest not avoiding a process relates to the fact that most jurisdictions have what is called "actual notice" or "constructive notice" exceptions to the personal service rule. If a process server cannot notify you by handing you a piece of paper, a plaintiff's attorney can simply file a notice of claim in an appropriate local publication of general circulation for a designated period. For instance, your local newspaper can provide appropriate notice to any given individual under most circumstances. If the plaintiff's attorney satisfies the service of process rules under the local jurisdiction, they can then apply for a "default judgment," if you do not file an "answer" within an appropriate period.

If you happen to be insured, an insurance company may decide that you are not insured because you avoided service of process and allowed a default judgment to be entered against you. Default judgment allows a plaintiff to appear in court and have a judge determine that you admit all of the allegations of negligence against you. A judgment will be entered and the plaintiff's attorney will then present a statement of damages. In the face of an undisputed statement of damages, most courts will simply accept the plaintiff's argument that the full amount of the damages alleged should be assessed against you.

Once damages are assessed pursuant to a default judgment, a plaintiff and his or her attorney may simply begin garnishment proceedings against you. Garnishment proceedings can take many different forms. However, the most simple form of garnishment involves a seizure of any money contained within your bank accounts, as well as the seizure of any paychecks you have coming from your employer. Liens against real property you own may also be imposed.

Let me give you this assurance: We can find you. Lawyers have resources that allow us to identify where you live, where you bank, and where you work. We can subpoena you to attend a debtor's examination wherein you must disgorge all information relating to any liquid assets you might have available. Once a lawyer discovers what liquid assets you have available, those assets are subject to seizure. There are exceptions, including your employer-provided 401k; however, my point is that it would be futile for you to avoid service of process.

Please trust me when I say that no one can avoid the law. There are simply too many resources available to licensed attorneys about individuals who are attempting to avoid service of process and liability. Of course, there are exceptions to every rule. If someone is "judgment proof," for instance, it means he or she has no liquid assets and he or she is probably unemployed. That said, most people will have some sort of liquid asset available and are probably employed.

It is also noteworthy that, once a judgment is entered against you, the attorney or plaintiff who has sued you has the ability to re-enter the judgment against you until the end of time. Most judgments are good for between ten to fifteen years. Each of those ten to fifteen year judgments can be re-entered in any court in the United States, and you will be subject to garnishment for as long as you live.

So, it is worthwhile for any particular named defendant to simply accept service of process and notify their insurance carrier of any complaint that has been filed against them. If there is no insurance, then you will have other issues to deal with that will require the assistance of a lawyer.

The fact of the matter is, statutes and rules of procedure were made to protect all parties in every civil lawsuit. They are not simply geared to allow plaintiffs to collect as much money from you as possible. They are also there to protect a defendant's interests and, by avoiding service of process, you are simply avoiding protections that the law provides named defendants. In fact, most jurisdictions will have a uniform jury instruction that instructs all jurors hearing your case to assume that a defendant has not violated the law. You should use the law to your advantage, and a lawyer will know how to assist their client in maximizing the advantages any given law provides.

Once you have been served, as scary as this may seem, most people in this country will be able to fight against the allegations of negligence or other tort that have been raised against him. There is a certain period, usually twenty to thirty days after service, within which a defendant can respond to a complaint that has been filed in any jurisdictional court. Certain things must be alleged in an "answer" to preserve certain defenses that might completely "bar" (or prevent) the ability of any plaintiff to collect money from them. These defenses that must be pled in an official "answer" are known as "affirmative defenses." Any lawyer worth his or her salt will know exactly what these affirmative defenses are and whether they apply in any given case. Affirmative defenses that are available will be addressed in subsequent chapters. That said, if you happen to be a defendant, it is advisable for you to simply accept service and tender the matter to your insurance company. That insurance company will, in turn, send the matter to one of their defense attorneys who will vigorously represent your interests.

In protecting those interests, a defense attorney will want to speak with any named defendant as quickly as possible, securing any and all evidence that might be used to prevent liability from attaching to their client.

Becoming a Plaintiff

If you have the benefit of being a plaintiff, hopefully you have obtained the assistance of counsel. In addition, with any luck, you have actually hired someone who knows what they are doing. It may take many months for your lawyer to determine whether you have a cause of action. For that matter, they may determine that you actually have numerous causes of action available to you. However, there may be costs and benefits associated with each of those causes of action.

For instance, certain causes of action might allow for the recovery of attorney's fees. However, you should also ask your attorney whether those available attorney's fees are allowed to the "prevailing party." If they are, you should make sure that you have a strong basis for recovering on a claim subject to a prevailing party's attorney fee statute. If you do not, your attorney will have to explain to you that the claim is risky and you might end up being responsible for the defendant's attorney's fees in the event that your lawyer cannot satisfy your burden of proof and you lose the case at trial.

Certain claims of a technical nature may even involve the hiring of experts to give your lawyer the assurance he or she might need in bringing the claim on your behalf. Be aware of the fact that experts are not cheap. Experts come in all shapes and sizes. There might be medical experts, accident reconstruction experts, forensic experts of all types, engineers, and economists. Whatever the case may be, these experts cost money. The better and more reliable your expert, the more likely it is that your claim will be successful. Of course, hiring a superior expert in any particular discipline will cost more money than hiring a professional witness or other "hired gun."

Hired guns take two particular forms: (1) someone who has testified many, many times and will do their best to justify a claim; and/or (2) individuals who are at the top of their game, well respected in their particular discipline, and experienced witnesses. Of course, the latter type of expert is preferred. Defense lawyers know the difference. The more respected your lawyer and expert happens to be, the more likely it is that you will be able to settle the case in advance of trial.

Whatever the case may be, the evaluation and analysis of your claim will take time. Your attorney will need to evaluate whether it is reasonable and appropriate for them to actually "invest in your case" by hiring good and reliable experts. They will need an opportunity to review whatever documentation is available and have that documentation reviewed by individuals outside of their practice in various areas of specialty. Rare is the case where you will walk into a plaintiff's lawyer's office, have them review your case and present you with a settlement check within a matter of months. It simply does not happen that way. You should be prepared for a long process extending anywhere from six months in the most simple of cases to one to four years for more complex matters. The higher the case value, the longer it may take to recover by way of settlement or verdict.

Depending upon the jurisdiction you are subject to, your lawyer should be able to give you a general estimation about how long the litigation process might take in your case. If this is not offered, you should ask. This will help alleviate your concerns and anxiety associated with the inevitable "waiting game" that occurs during the course of almost every lawsuit.

Becoming a Defendant

Some people who are sued could not care less about the fact that they have been named in a lawsuit. Others, on the other hand, are probably more concerned about liability and "exposure." If you have purchased this book, it is likely that you belong to the group covered under the latter description.

Assuming you have already been served and that you have presented those documents to any available insurance carrier you might have at your disposal, your lawyer will want to meet with you to discuss the facts of the case. In this event, you should bring with you to your initial conference any and all documentation you might have relevant to the case. I have also armed you with questions and information in the previous chapters that you should pursue.

Once the case has been handed over to a lawyer, the ball is in their court. Most rules of procedure provide your lawyer an opportunity to notify the opposing attorney of their involvement. Once this occurs, it would be unethical for the plaintiff's attorney or anyone associated with the plaintiff's attorney to contact you. There should be no telephone calls or other inquiries relating to this lawsuit from anyone other than your lawyer or the law firm he or she happens to work with.

It often takes some time for the defense attorney to understand the facts of the case and nuances associated with the claims that have been raised against you. Do not hold back. Do not hide any information that might be damaging to you or your case.

For instance, if you have ever been convicted of a crime, DUI or otherwise, let your lawyer know. Inform your attorney about other cases in which you have been involved. If you provided sworn testimony in any court of law or any other case, let them know.

The lawyer who is defending you has heard it all. For you to receive an appropriate defense, that lawyer needs to be aware of everything that might be relevant to the case and even many details that might not be relevant. Ugly divorces or custody proceedings, past convictions of any kind of offense or crime are all fair game. Only when your lawyer is armed with the facts and the relevant history can they plan accordingly and protect you from any unforeseen events that might rise up and threaten to "expose" you even more than you already are.

For the most part, there are usually rules of evidence or procedure that can be used to protect defendants. Only when your defense lawyer is informed of all negative aspects of your claim and background can they shield you from the stress and embarrassment of those "skeletons."

Clients of mine sometimes wonder whether I am their attorney or the insurance company's attorney. The reality and ultimate truth is that I am both. However, a defense lawyer must always be thinking and arguing in the best interests of the defendant. Defense lawyers are your advisor, your confidant, and your advocate. Regardless of what the facts might be, we will always argue those facts vigorously and conclusively in your favor. You should not fear the truth. A defense lawyer is always on your side.

It has often been said, and I believe it is true, that trial lawyers are born and not bred. A good trial lawyer will invest themselves personally and emotionally in your case, while maintaining an objective viewpoint. This is a special skill that most, but not all, trial lawyers possess. We are creative and intuitive. We look for the story behind the story. We want to live your reality and place ourselves exactly in your shoes at the time and place of the events in question. Not only does this involve a deep and detailed understanding of the facts, it also involves an understanding of your personality, psyche, and view of the world. Only when you help us understand these details will we be able to appropriately defend each and every attack that might eventually surface.

Summary

This is the beginning of the road. It is not easy for either party to travel. Your lawyer is there as a guide and as your defender. We will take the lead and help you through the difficult obstacles each and every party must overcome. Clients that are willing to accept this, explain the truth, and provide perspective will be the most satisfied. Nevertheless, we are not there to simply tell you what you want to hear. It is imperative that every trial attorney stay objective, viewing all facts and circumstances as though through the eyes of a layperson and juror. Sometimes, you will like what you hear. Other times, you will be afraid or offended. Whatever the case may be, your attorney should be able to provide you with a plan or strategy for each and every particular issue that might arise in a case. It is impossible for every lawyer to explain their inner-workings or strategies, secondary strategies or reservations. Oftentimes, the moves we make as trial lawyers are based upon intangible and "gut feelings" about the people and parties we are dealing with at any given time. Working on instinct, it is almost second nature for us to evaluate the various legal workings at play. Our judge, opposing counsel, witnesses, evidence, and jurisdiction all play a role in how we choose to handle any given situation. This is why it is so important for you to appropriately select a lawyer to represent your interests. This is why trust forms the foundation of any attorney-client relationship. Without it, your interests are not totally and completely protected.

5

The Professionals

While engaged in litigation, you will be involved with a number of individuals, each of whom plays a special role in the litigation process. What follows is a general discussion of the players with whom you may come into contact.

The Defense Team

A typical defense team consists of the "first chair" trial lawyer and his or her staff. First chair lawyers tend to be partners in the firm or senior level associates. This is driven by the complexity of the case and potential damages exposure. In other words, cases that are worth a significant amount of money generally necessitate a higher level of experience.

Within most firms, there is a stratified system based on seniority and time in practice. Senior partners, mid-level partners, and junior partners occupy the first tier. Second-tier attorneys would include senior associates, mid-level associates, and junior associates.

Mid-level and junior associates will generally not handle cases in a "first chair" position. They are essentially the soldiers and ground troops who get down to the nitty gritty. They file routine motions and track discovery. Sometimes, they will interview witnesses and experts, and they might even conduct generally inconsequential depositions.

Senior level associates will typically have between six and nine years of experience. They may sit as first chair trial lawyers in medium- to low-end damages cases, but many will be "second chair" trial lawyers who are getting the necessary experience to one day sit in the first chair at trial. As second chair, they may take a few minor witnesses, organize exhibits and witnesses, argue trial motions, and provide as needed assistance to the first chair. They provide a direct line of communication to the first chair lawyer when he or she is hard to reach.

All partners should be first chair lawyers. Any lawyer who makes partner without the ability to serve as first chair should not be a partner. Regardless of level within the partnership tier, these lawyers have proven themselves to the other partners in the firm. They have demonstrated competence on all levels of case management and have "passed the test" imposed on them by the other partners and clients.

High-end cases will generally be managed by both a partner and an associate. The bigger the case, the more people there will be working on it as the days go by. The first chair partner will be responsible for primary strategy decisions, retaining quality experts, identifying key discovery and creating the "theme" of the defense case. The presentation of witnesses must be woven, as best as possible, into a multilayered story that the jury will identify with and understand. He or she will take all key depositions of witnesses and maintain personal contact with the client every step of the way.

Paralegals

Paralegals have a varying range of responsibilities, depending on the first chair attorney's individual needs, expectations, and comfort level. Paralegals are not lawyers. However, a skilled paralegal has a wide range of authority. Some draft legal documents, such as subpoenas and notices and many are able to keep track of litigation in such a way that the trial lawyer has an easier time staying on top of discovery. It is not uncommon for paralegals to have direct contact with clients, since they rarely leave the office and are generally available at times when a lawyer may not be. Either way, a paralegal can form an integral part of any litigation team.

In my particular practice, the paralegal is often the first individual to lay eyes on the discovery in the case. Their first obligation is to review the discovery and ensure that all appropriate materials that had been previously requested were produced by the opposing side. Any holes or omissions in the documents provided are highlighted and brought to the attention of the trial lawyer. The records are organized in an orderly fashion, paginated, and distributed to whoever might need to review that particular set of records. For instance, financial documentation will generally go out to an expert economist. Medical records will be provided to any medical experts that have been retained. Any other key documentation will be highlighted and brought to the trial attorney's attention.

In cases involving a large volume of records, it is often the paralegal's responsibility to assemble those records and create a "chronology" of the care or events at issue in the case. When dealing with individual records on a piecemeal basis, it is often helpful to look at the events detailed on a single document, rather than sifting through hundreds of pages in an effort to recreate a timeline. Some chronologies are abbreviated, others are very detailed. For instance, in a birth injury case, it is often important to prepare a minute-by-minute event log in an effort to determine exactly when things happened, what the patient's vital signs were, what every nurse was doing at every particular moment, where the doctor was, etc.

As I often instruct associates at my law firm, knowledge is supreme. A lawyer with a good solid understanding of the facts and events in every case will have the upper hand during the course of litigation. Mistaken or incorrect assumptions about what happened at what time is oftentimes the difference between victory and defeat at trial. In this regard, a solid paralegal is one of the trial lawyer's best weapons utilized in defending or prosecuting a case.

Legal Assistant

A legal assistant or legal secretary is the trial lawyer's "right hand." Trial lawyers and their legal assistants often have close working relationships, primarily out of necessity. To properly manage a busy law practice, an experienced legal assistant is paramount. He or she will be able to keep an additional set of eyes on every case coming in the door. They often maintain the lawyer's daily schedule of events and a "tickle system" whereby deadlines and other triggering events might be raised in timely manner to the trial lawyer.

Highly experienced legal assistants are few and far between and, it is often said among practicing lawyers, they are "worth their weight in gold." They are often the first contact any client will have with the lawyer's office. They must be capable of managing a wide variety of details that come with any lawsuit. This would include everything from understanding the rules of procedure, appropriate methods of service, timelines and deadlines associated with every conceivable legal document to be filed with the court, the attorney's personal trial docket, and witness availability in any given case. In a busy law practice, time management is absolutely critical and the legal assistant's ability to exercise good judgment and common sense together with a highly developed sense of interpersonal and social skills is crucial. Most attorneys stay away from the word "secretary" when referring to their legal assistant because a legal assistant is more than a secretary. Although they handle dictation and typing, as well as scheduling issues, a legal assistant is far more than a transcriptionist and they are especially skilled in handling lawsuits and the court system.

Law Clerk

Law clerks are generally only utilized in larger firms. Typically, a law clerk is a second or third year law student who is attempting to obtain practical experience and make connections within the legal community prior to taking the state bar examination.

A law clerk will generally have little to no client contact. Their primary responsibilities are to engage in limited research at the direction of the trial attorneys working on the case. Some law clerks, depending upon the type of case they are handling, will have a wide range of responsibilities. However, in most firms specializing in civil litigation, a law clerk's role is fairly minimal, intentionally so. They are "lawyers in training," and require a great deal of supervision.

Insurance Claims Adjuster or Specialist

Once a party is served with a legal document, if no lawyer has been retained, a defendant should notify any applicable insurance carriers. At that point, a claims agent/adjuster/specialist will be assigned to the matter and will contact the insured party. Communications between the claims agent and the insured party are privileged and confidential. You should confirm this with the adjuster before you provide any statements.

The claims person will then assign one of their insurance defense law firms to the suit and provide the insured with instructions about what they can expect. The lawyer's name may be assigned by the law firm's internal claims management partner, who will then decide in conjunction with the claims adjuster which attorney within the firm is specially suited to handle the new lawsuit.

Throughout the duration of the lawsuit, the claims adjuster will remain involved and is responsible for moving the suit along, reviewing regular status reports from the assigned lawyer, and evaluating strategy issues as the case progresses. They will remain available to the insured throughout the process.

Process Servers

In most states, process servers are essentially a group of specialized delivery people who are paid to "serve" lawyers and parties in litigation. Once service has been accomplished and a defendant has been placed on notice of the lawsuit by these individuals, there is no longer a need to continue utilizing a professional process server, as the defendant will usually "lawyer up." Once the attorney has been retained, as an officer of the court, all documents should be channeled through that lawyer. Service on the lawyer by regular or electronic mail satisfies service requirements in most jurisdictions.

Service of process can also be accomplished utilizing the local county sheriff, if the county court is being utilized. This is often a less expensive alternative, but service duties take a back seat to police work. So, if prompt or rush service is needed, a professional process server should be utilized.

Judges

Judges come in all shapes and sizes. Some are highly experienced trial judges who have been on the bench for many years and handle a variety of litigation including negligence, defamation, employment cases, probate, family law, and many other myriad of subspecialty cases within civil litigation. Although it should probably not be the case, every judge brings with them to the bench their personal experiences and biases. To pretend that all judges are the same and all parties are equal in the eyes of the law would be naïve. The fact is, getting the right or wrong judge will either make or break your case. Encountering a series of poor rulings could be devastating to a trial attorney's strategy.

Let us face it, not all people have the same level of intellect and capacity. Some judges stepped into the position as a matter of political appointment or public service. Others saw the opportunity as one that would enable them to change existing law or allow them to impose their own sense of justice in any given case. For the most part, I have had a good experience with trial judges handling my cases. It is my firm belief, however, that this is the result of the type of cases I actually handle. The more complex the case, the more likely it is you will end up with an experienced trial judge. Judges with seniority and standing within the judiciary will often have the ability to select the cases they want to preside over. Routine, run of the mill auto accidents, slips and falls, DUIs, etc., are probably not at the top of the list when it comes to a judge's interest level in overseeing the case. On the other hand, complex medical cases, products liability, high-end discrimination cases and the like are generally coveted by judges. The higher profile the case, the more likely it is that the matter is being handled by experienced trial lawyers, which also makes the judge's job a lot easier. The parties to a case will generally attempt to streamline complex issues as best as possible prior to walking into the courtroom. Many exhibits have probably already been discussed between the opposing sides and agreed upon. Resources, such as a video technician or IT specialist will sometimes be shared by the lawyers working on the case. Experienced lawyers know what to expect and know what is expected of them by trial court judges.

On occasion, the parties will know who their trial judge is months in advance of trial. It is likely that both sides will conduct a thorough investigation, to the extent necessary, of any trial judge hearing their case. Understanding the personal experiences and political leanings of any particular judge is critical.

Judicial Clerk

Every judge has a judicial clerk. Judicial clerks are much like law clerks in a law firm; however, they can be generally appointed for a longer period. Some are law students; others are newly admitted attorneys. For instance, most federal judges will be working with a newly admitted attorney for a two- or three-year period.

The judicial clerk is also an important person to be respectful of. Before a case comes to trial, the judicial clerk will often be the "filter" the judge relies on in reaching determinations on any motion arguments and so on. It is not uncommon for the judicial clerk to actually write out the judge's "written opinions" on complex legal motions before the court pretrial. They also may have a large hand in drafting pre-trial and post-trial orders and rulings. No one working with a judge is "inconsequential." They are there because the judge trusts/respects them. Act accordingly.

Judicial Assistants

A judicial assistant (JA) acts much like a legal assistant for a law firm. They are responsible for managing the judge's calendar, scheduling events, and work as a filter or gatekeeper for the judge.

JAs can provide parties with helpful pretrial information. It is not uncommon for a trial lawyer or their staff to contact the judicial assistant in an effort to determine how the judge likes his or her courtroom to be set up, special rules that might apply, when the judge wants to see trial documents, etc.

Being a lawyer is often about following and understanding all the rules. There are state and federal rules of procedure, local rules within each particular court, and even special rules of procedure that apply in each judge's individual courtroom. Your attorney should have a grasp of all conceivable rules that might apply in a case up to and through trial. The JA is one of the best people to work with in determining the scope of any particular rules the judge specifically enforces or applies in their courtroom.

Arbitrators

In some jurisdictions, the use of arbitrators is favored. Arbitrators are often working lawyers who have passed a series of requirements and have been appointed by the bench to oversee certain cases. The necessity for utilizing arbitrators has risen over the years in response to an increasing number of lawsuits accompanied by the diminishing court budgets or judicial budgets.

In some jurisdictions, there are statutes requiring arbitration in cases that do not exceed a certain dollar value. There are also arbitration agreements that can be enforced, which require arbitration. That said, arbitration is simply an alternative to a formal jury or bench trial. Most state statutes that do require arbitration for certain cases (based on dollar value) are immediately appealable for a jury trial.

Typically, the arbitrator is someone who is either appointed by the court automatically or appointed by the parties who have mutually agreed to the use of an arbitrator and the specific arbitrator who has been chosen. In some instances, there may be a "panel arbitration," which is typically comprised of three members. In those cases, each party will select its own arbitrator. Those two arbitrators will then select a third arbitrator. At the time of the arbitration, a majority of the arbitrators will then decide the verdict and damages, if any.

Mediators

Mediators can be used during the course of a lawsuit as a way of reaching settlement and compromise. Most mediators are either retired judges or trial attorneys who have established themselves in the community as being fair and reasonable. It is imperative that whoever is selected as a mediator be respected by both sides.

Mediators are being used more and more often and are favored, in many cases, by insurance companies. The typical "back and forth" negotiation between a plaintiff's lawyer and a defense lawyer is unfortunately becoming rare.

In many instances, mediators have the ability to serve as a "buffer" between the two or more sides to reach an amicable resolution, short of trial. Retired judges might be particularly persuasive in certain cases because they can give the respective parties a real life view of what actually happens or can happen during the course of trial. Selection of a mediator and the timing of scheduling mediation, if any, are within the sole discretion of the trial attorney.

If mediation is recommended, your lawyer should be able to provide you with their strategy reasons for doing so, as well as the names of mediators who might be helpful. For instance, it is not uncommon for me, as a defense lawyer, to have to deal with a plaintiff who has unreasonable expectations about the value of their case. Every plaintiff thinks their case is worth millions of dollars. If the defense lawyer has done a good job of working with their client, their client should have an idea about where jury verdicts have been falling relative to the issues in their case. If I feel as though the plaintiff's lawyer or their client is overestimating the value of their case, it is not uncommon for me to agree to have the case mediated by an experienced plaintiff's lawyer who will be able to discuss with the plaintiff and their lawyer the realities associated with liability and valuation. If I hear from a plaintiff's lawyer whom I trust that I am undervaluing a case or overestimating my case's defensibility, I might also recommend settling the case for more than originally suggested.

As time goes on, less and less cases are making it to trial. One of the reasons for this relates to the fact that mediators and mediation are becoming standard operating procedure for civil cases.

It is noteworthy that some jurisdictions actually require alternative dispute resolution (ADR) before allowing a trial. Mediation is one type of ADR. A judicial settlement conference is another. However, it has been my experience that mediations are often more successful than judicial settlement conferences. You should ask your attorney whether ADR is a requirement in your jurisdiction and, if so, whether this is something you should expect down the road.

Court Reporter

A court reporter is an individual who is specially trained in recording discussions or testimony in shorthand on a special device. Most court reporters now use a computerized system that will enable them to create and keep an accurate record of any court proceedings or depositions. A court reporter also has the ability, as a notary public, to administer the oath to a witness before testimony and to authenticate their trial/deposition transcripts as an "official court record."

IT Specialist

In complex cases, it is not unusual for the litigation team to consist of support staff, including IT specialists. The ability to communicate complex information to a panel of lay jurors is difficult without the use of modern technology. As trial draws near, your trial attorney may encourage the use of certain specialists who are skilled at preparing presentations, summaries of evidence, computer diagrams, graphs and charts, etc.

These computer-generated images can be formatted in a way that your trial attorney will have the best chance of communicating their strategy so the jury will understand the principles behind it. On occasion, your trial attorney will be working with an information technology specialist from the beginning of the case forward. Documents are provided to the technologist, and those documents are scanned into a master system, which enables the specialist to pull up individual documents, mark them accordingly, highlight, magnify, or otherwise manipulate those documents in such a way that your trial attorney will be able to emphasize key points of their case for both the judge and/or jury.

Because information technology specialists are fairly expensive to utilize, not all attorneys will have the ability to hire someone to help them with these aspects of the case. In the event the case is a complex or high value matter, however, IT specialists are commonplace.

If you are interested, you as the client should have the ability to request graphs and make suggestions to your lawyer concerning how to effectively communicate strategy and key facts. The lawyer will have the final say; but, a lawyer who does not utilize his own client's knowledge and expertise is probably working with a handicap. Some lawyers, like myself, give their clients the option of becoming more or less involved in the litigation as time passes. You should not be afraid to voice your own opinions about your case and perhaps more effective ways of communicating complex information to your selected jury or judge.

Trial Consultants

Trial consultants are most often retained by defense counsel. However, their role is not limited in this respect. Many high-end plaintiff attorneys or those handling mass torts will utilize trial consultants during the course of litigation.

Trial consultants often have a background or specialized training in human psychology and sociology. They are paid to analyze case issues and potential jurors. Their opinions are then used to assist the lawyer in either shaping the presentation of their case or in selecting the best jury pool.

High value cases might also be set for a "focus group." A focus group is essentially an abbreviated presentation of the case facts to a large group of individuals who have been randomly selected in the community. The groups can be run any number of ways. Most often, they involve a presentation of the evidence and argument from the lead trial lawyer and another lawyer within the same firm. One will represent the plaintiff, and the other will present the defendant's best case.

At the conclusion of those presentations, the group will be separated into mock juries, and their deliberations will be watched, recorded, and analyzed. From these focus groups it is often possible to identify both "problem issues" and effective arguments. The mock juror's personal backgrounds and their stance on the issues might also assist the trial attorney in selecting the real jury at the time of trial. For instance, do we want military veterans on our jury? What about teachers? Would a fifty to sixty-year-old, middle-income female be a good choice?

The information gleaned from these evaluations is then evaluated and potential juror profiles can be created. Whether that profile is accurate or not will remain to be seen until the verdict is delivered by the jury foreperson.

6

Understanding Basic Legalese

Throughout the duration of your lawsuit, many legal terms of art will be mentioned and discussed over the course of time as your case progresses. It is not uncommon for lawyers to use these terms as a matter of course and, sometimes, without remembering that you are new to the process. It is your lawyer's obligation to explain in detail the significance of these terms of art and what they have to do with your case.

Statutes Limiting Lawsuits

When deciding whether a case will be filed or whether a case has certain defenses that can be utilized against the allegations and claim, there are several issues that are considered by every lawyer. First and foremost, every lawyer must determine whether a case has been brought too late. Every state has enacted statutes that prevent lawsuits or claims from lingering too long. These statutes are called *statutes of limitations* and *statutes of ultimate repose*. They are two ideas that relate to the same concept.

Statutes of limitations vary from case to case and from claim to claim. Not every state has the same statute of limitations period that would apply to a particular claim. There are also many caveats contained within the rules and case law that will affect whether a statute of limitations has run.

By way of example, many states have a two-year statute of limitations associated with personal injury claims. In other words, if I am rear-ended in my car and injured on January 1, 2013, I must file my lawsuit no later than January 1, 2015. This is a very easy example of a statute of limitations. Nuances associated with statutes of limitation are significant, however, and many times the start date for a statute of limitations is difficult to determine.

In medical cases, for instance, many states have enacted "*discovery rules*." A discovery rule simply allows an injured party to delay running of the statute of limitations until they "discover" they have a cause of action. As an example, assume Patient A has been followed by a primary care doctor for many years. For the last three years, Patient A has had an undiagnosed lung cancer. However, during the course of the last three years, Patient A has been complaining to his or her primary care physician of cancer-related symptoms. In fact, tests were taken three years prior to the diagnosis that should have led a reasonably prudent physician to diagnose the cancer or at least recommend further testing that would have led to that diagnosis. If there is a general statute of limitations of only two years, Patient A would be precluded from suing his or her primary care doctor for conduct that occurred longer ago than that time. However, under the discovery rule, the two-year statute of limitations would not commence until the patient discovers he or she has been harmed. Once told of the diagnosis, Patient A will have a responsibility to engage in appropriate investigation in determining whether he or she has a cause of action against their physician, and the two-year statute will begin running once they learn of their diagnosis.

On the other hand, a "statute of ultimate repose" constitutes the absolute maximum time a patient or injured party has to bring a lawsuit. As the name implies, these filing date cut-offs are also created in statute. Statutes of ultimate repose will vary from state to state and can be as short as three years or as long as fifteen years. Some states may have even longer statutes of ultimate repose. A significant number of states, however, have a five-year and a ten-year statute of ultimate repose. Certain professionals, like physicians, are given the benefit of a shorter statute of ultimate repose as a method of insulating the profession from an open-ended liability risk.

So, let us use the example described above with Patient A. Assume that the care at issue in the above example did not occur three years prior to the date of discovery. Instead, it occurred six years prior to the date of discovery and there is a five-year statute of ultimate repose in place. Under those circumstances, even though Patient A's cancer was not discovered until six years after the care rendered, he or she would still be prevented (or barred) from bringing the lawsuit, if the only care at issue occurred six years earlier.

Of course, other exceptions might apply and other rules might be utilized in helping Patient A get over the statute of limitations/repose hurdle. However, that is what your lawyer is for. There are entire books written on the statute of limitations and the nuances associated with the statutory language. There are exceptions, such as the "*continuing course of treatment doctrine*" and *actual notice* rules. There are also rules associated with claims being brought on behalf of minors or disabled people. Fraudulent conduct will also toll the repose statute.

Nevertheless, this should give you a bird's eye view of the general issues involved with statutory claim limitations. In many cases, the analysis will be easy. In others, the arguments are very subtle and require experience and expertise.

Venue

The term "venue" refers to the available choice of courts. A venue can be any number of courts, including state, federal, or specialty courts, such as an admiralty court or tribal court. The two most frequently utilized venues for trying tort cases are either the state or federal court system.

In the majority of circumstances, your average personal injury tort case will be brought in a state circuit or superior court. In the state court context, venue generally refers to the county in which a claim may be brought. Different counties will have an effect on case value and defensibility. Much as a judge can affect a case, your jury pool will also have a substantial impact on both value and defensibility. As a rule of thumb, the more rural a jury, the more likely a defense verdict will occur. If a plaintiff's verdict does occur in a rural jurisdiction, the values also tend to be less. However, make no mistake, there are no cut and dried rules when it comes to juries. Nevertheless, statistically speaking, if you were to compare the plaintiff and defense verdicts and the typical jury verdict damages awards in any particular county, you would probably see this trend.

Defensibility and valuation, however, are not the only considerations a lawyer must weigh. Case complexity also comes into play from time to time. More educated jurors tend to live in metropolitan areas. Very few professionals reside far from the city. This has nothing to do with intelligence. Instead, it relates to the level of education and the jurors' experience in dealing with complicated information on a routine basis.

Sometimes federal courts will be available. However, many states have different federal districts located within their borders. Oftentimes, when dealing with a federal court case, selection of the appropriate district is jurisdictional and largely based upon the location of the defendants or place in which the injury occurred. This is typical of most cases. In cases involving general torts, venue is limited based upon either where the tort occurred or where one or more of the defendants reside.

Types of Law

Your lawyer will have to analyze various types of law in either prosecuting or defending your lawsuit. Types of law include state or federal statutes, case law, common law, rules of procedure, rules of evidence, code of federal regulations (CFRs), state and federal constitutional law, and a myriad other obscure forms of law. For the most part, trial lawyers deal primarily with statutes and case law.

Statutes refer to codified legislative enactments. In other words, they are the rules of the state that are created by the people we elect in the House and the Senate. Oftentimes, the legislature will essentially "punt" some of their obligations to a specialized committee. The legislatures will enact a general law, and then appoint a department within the government to create, enact, and enforce a number of *regulations*. In most federal court situations, these are referred to as CFRs. The statute may provide for the general framework; however, individuals and businesses are often subject to even more specific rules set out under the CFRs.

Case law involves court decisions that have been published in the state and federal reporters. Only written decisions prepared by certain courts will be reported. For instance, as far as state laws are concerned, only cases decided by the Oregon Supreme Court or Oregon Court of Appeals will be published in the Oregon reporters. Furthermore, not all opinions that are written by the courts are published. Only a select number of cases the courts decide they want to publish will be considered authoritative law. Trial court decisions are never published. Of course, the caveat would be that the Court of Appeals and Supreme Court cases are generally trial court cases that have been heard and decided by a trial court judge. Nevertheless, decisions made by a trial court judge are not binding on parties in subsequent cases and cannot be cited, typically, in briefs that are submitted to the court in other matters. They may, from time to time, be used in support of an argument as what an attorney may hope is "persuasive" on the issue. Nevertheless, relying upon unpublished decisions or decisions that were made in other trial court cases is typically disfavored. In fact, unpublished Court of Appeals and Supreme Court cases in the state <u>cannot</u> be cited, and their opinions specifically state this.

Of course, to prepare a case for trial, the lawyers must follow *civil rules of procedure* and other statutory rules to engage in the discovery process and prepare the necessary filings for court. Although rules of procedure and *rules of evidence* will vary from state to state and court to court, for the most part, they are substantially similar. Most state court rules of procedure, for instance, are based largely on the federal rules of civil procedure. Likewise, rules of evidence are also based in large part on the federal rules of evidence.

When a lawyer refers to a "common law cause of action," they are referring to a long-established rule of law developed in England. These general principles or "*common laws*" traveled with the English colonists to the United States and embedded themselves in the fabric of our society. For instance, the law of negligence is a common law principle.

On the other hand, there are also *principles of equity*, which can also be enforceable laws. In the United States, we do not have both courts of equity and courts of law. Instead, any court can hear claims brought in equity or in law.

Equitable claims are based upon the principles of fairness. One common example might be a claim for breach of contract. The equitable claim of estoppel or unjust enrichment can be brought against someone where there is no written contract in place. The idea is that, simply because there is no written contract, this does not mean that one party should be unjustly enriched by the other.

The law of adverse possession is a fairly typical example of an equitable claim as well. Adverse possession involves a situation where, typically, two sets of neighbors believe that they each own a certain parcel of land. One of those neighbors invests time and expense into property, but is under the mistaken belief that the property is theirs. Adverse possession comes into play when the true property owner decides to evict their neighbor as a trespasser. (This is not the only way adverse possession works; it is merely an example.) The premise is that the legal property holder should not enjoy the fruits of the labors of the errant property owner in the event that the neighbor, who has invested all of his time and expense, has done so for a period of many years. In other words, where there is no remedy in law, the court can create an "equitable" remedy to deal with the situation.

7

Dealing with Parties and the Media

The vast majority of lawsuits will attract absolutely zero attention from anyone, including the media. However, there are a number of cases that might arise that are considered "high profile" or "media-worthy" lawsuits. From time to time, news agencies will contact either a party to a lawsuit or their lawyer.

The Media

It is my strong suggestion that you do not speak with the media under any circumstance. This book is meant to be a no-nonsense guide to understanding the litigation process. So, at the risk of offending journalists out there, experience has shown that journalists contact individuals after they have already decided the type and tone of story they wish to write. If what you have to say supports their view, they will include one or more of your "quotes." If what you have to say does not support their viewpoint, they will quote you anyway and make it sound as though you support their story. It has been my personal experience that news reporters do not "listen" to what you have to say. Inevitably, what you are quoted as saying will be incorrect, slanted, taken out of context, or any number of variables for them to "fit" it into their story. So, please let your attorney handle media contact. Anything you say can and will be used against you later. It is, quite honestly, not worth the gamble trusting a reporter to understand your case and print a story in such a way that gives you any benefit.

If you are contacted by the media, you should simply refer that individual to your lawyer. In all likelihood, the official response will be "no comment whatsoever." There are rare cases where a press release or some news interview is warranted and may make strategic sense to your lawyer. However, rarely, if ever, does a news report improve a litigant's chances of either having a case dismissed, settled, or otherwise expedited.

Over the years, I have had many occasions to rub elbows with journalists. None of my experiences have been good. Quite honestly, even the stories that were favorable to my clients still created obstacles for me to overcome as their trial lawyer in selecting a jury and litigating their case.

Adverse Parties

Once you are sued by someone, or you decide to file a lawsuit against an individual or group of individuals, it does not make any sense whatsoever to communicate with those individuals at all. This is what you hired your lawyer to do. There are specific rules governing how attorneys communicate with opposing counsel and the parties they represent. There is nothing to be gained by deciding to play Sherlock Holmes and do additional investigation or snooping into witnesses or parties. Also, anything you do, say, or discover is likely <u>not</u> protected by a privilege and must be disclosed at a deposition or other form of discovery inquiry.

If you have suggestions or ideas, it is best to forward those on to your lawyer, so that he or she can make a determination as to whether additional investigation or interviews are warranted. There is nothing wrong with offering to speak with certain individuals, but leave it up to your lawyer to decide whether that contact would be helpful, is legal, or a reasonable idea. Again, your comments and behavior can and will be reported by other individuals and it may or may not be spun into an unfavorable account of what really occurred. It is simply best to stay away from individuals involved with the lawsuit, unless you cannot help it.

Witnesses

A "witness" is essentially anyone who knows anything whatsoever about the case or issues related to the case. Witnesses can be family members, employers, co-workers, social acquaintances, and friends, even your local postman. With this in mind, it is in your interest and their interests that you not discuss the details of your case with anyone. Exactly who you can speak with and what you can say about the case should be discussed with your lawyer. For instance, there are generally privileges that allow a husband and a wife to talk without fear of that information being discovered. Nevertheless, there are exceptions to every rule, and you should be careful when discussing the details of your case.

One of the first questions that the opposing lawyer will ask of you when you happen to be deposed is whether you have discussed the details of your case with anyone. If you answer "yes," there will be additional questions in follow-up while that attorney determines whether they should take the time to investigate your communications with this third party in more detail. Those questions may or may not lead the other lawyer to interview your co-worker or whoever you spoke with and, potentially, demand their deposition. In other words, please do not create a headache for you or any of your friends, family, co-workers, etc.

Other Lawyers

The rules of professional conduct in every state prohibit any lawyer from speaking directly with a represented person about the details of the case in which they are involved. Once you are represented by a lawyer, no other lawyer is authorized to speak with you about the details of your lawsuit. Every lawyer must go through your lawyer to obtain information about the case. It is commonly referred to as unlawful "*ex parte* contact."

In this respect, it is also unlawful for any judge involved in your matter to speak with you outside the presence of counsel. Not only should you avoid speaking with a judge, but you also should not send letters to a judge or telephone a judge or the judge's clerk without notifying the adverse party or lawyer. Your lawyer knows these rules and there is really no reason for you to be in contact with the court once you are represented in any event. That said, *ex parte* contact could result in a disqualification of a good judge and should be avoided altogether.

The Judge

As mentioned above, if you are represented, you should have no direct contact with the judge. Your lawyer should handle any contact with the judge or his or her staff. If you are not represented, the rules of judicial conduct prevent the judge from having direct contact with you without all opposing attorneys being present. The judge's JA can provide you with instructions regarding how and under what circumstances the judge can be contacted directly.

8

The Discovery Process

As mentioned in previous chapters, "discovery" involves the process wherein both sides attempt to accumulate information about the lawsuit and its details. There are "discovery rules" set out under the rules of civil procedure in every state and federal jurisdiction. Discovery can and does take several forms. Without getting into complex details associated with strategy, I have simply outlined them for your review and consideration.

Requests for Production of Documents

A request for production is a very standard form of discovery request. In a request for production, the requesting attorney is simply asking for any documents, photos, e-mails, articles, or other physical, tangible items that might relate to the case. It is important to note that most jurisdictions allow the requesting attorneys to cast a very broad net when investigating a claim or lawsuit. In other words, the requested documentation or article need not be directly relevant to the claim. Instead, it should only be "likely to lead to the discovery of relevant evidence." In other words, even though the request for information or documentation does not seem to be relevant on its face, the discovery of that evidence may lead to the discovery of additional evidence that is, itself, independently relevant.

A request for production is probably one of the first types of discovery requests with which you will be involved. Your lawyer will receive one of these documents in the mail and will probably need to sit down and work with you in determining what, if any, materials you actually have. Most courts do not require litigants to "create" new documents or things that did not exist prior to the request. Additionally, there will be items that are simply no longer in existence or objectionable. Your attorney will need to determine whether objections can and should be raised in response to the requests for production that are received.

There is typically a thirty-day turnaround after receipt of a request for production. However, professional courtesies are extended between lawyers all of the time and it is relatively easy to obtain an extension of time within which to respond to the request.

In an accident case, most documents requested include photographs, medical records, journal entries, calendars, documentation relating to previous lawsuits, settlement agreements, insurance information, videotape, and myriad other documents and information. It is also typical, as explained in earlier chapters, for lawyers to demand access to hard drives and e-mails.

Interrogatories

Not all states utilize interrogatories. This type of discovery request is a set of written questions sent to the opposing attorney. These written questions ask opposing counsel to identify, in writing, names of witnesses, theories of the case, locations of documents, and a number of other details. Although most lawyers are generally able to answer these questions themselves, based upon the information they have already accumulated, your lawyer will also need to communicate with you about some of these details and how to appropriately respond to the interrogatories as they come in. As the name suggests, it is essentially an "interrogation" in writing.

Responses to interrogatories are considered to be statements given under oath and can, therefore, be used against any given party at trial. Many states require the party plaintiff or defendant to review and sign the document, certifying that the answers contained within it are truthful.

Requests for Admission

Requests for admission are very similar to interrogatories. However, requests for admission simply require the responding party to either "admit" or "deny" the questions presented. Most attorneys use requests for admission as a tool to reach agreement on certain issues with the opposing lawyer in advance of trial. For instance, I often use requests for admission prior to trial to confirm with an opposing lawyer that the documents I attach to the request are "authentic." If done correctly, this can eliminate the need for extraneous witnesses at trial, such as records custodians and so on.

Depositions

A deposition is one of the cornerstones of discovery utilized by trial lawyers in developing their trial strategy. A deposition allows the lawyer an opportunity to ask questions of any witness while under oath. That deposition can then be used as evidence at trial.

In most cases, a deposition is held in one of the lawyer's offices. I require that my clients be deposed in my own office, because of the preparation that we engage in and the fact that it is also more comfortable for my witness and myself. In other words, it is my "home court advantage."

There will be a court reporter present who will diligently type everything in shorthand on their stenography machine. It is the one and only opportunity for the opposing lawyer to ask questions of either you or some other witness prior to trial. It is also their one and only opportunity to essentially "size you up" as a witness and determine whether you are a threat to their case. I am a firm believer that trials are won and lost based on the strength of the respective witnesses. You can be a fabulous lawyer, but have terrible witnesses. Even if you happen to be one of the best trial lawyers in the world, but you have terrible witnesses, I would almost guarantee you that you will lose your lawsuit. On the other hand, I have also watched some of the worst lawyers present some of the best witnesses. These witnesses inevitably win the case. So, from the standpoint of a trial lawyer, how you present at your deposition will make all the difference in the world. It will be necessary for you to meet with your lawyer on one or more occasions to appropriately prepare you for your deposition. At that time, you will receive general instructions about how to deliver your testimony and how the deposition procedure should unfold.

Basic Instructions

As mentioned previously, a court reporter will be present at the deposition to swear you in and to type in shorthand every word exchanged during the course of the procedure. As a result, certain formalities are always encouraged. These formalities will also help reinforce some of the witness strategies discussed in the pages that follow.

The basic procedural tips are as follows:

1) A court reporter cannot type two people speaking at the same time. Therefore, you must not talk over the deposing attorney. Wait for the question before you begin answering.
2) Do not use "uh huh" or "huh uh" to answer questions. Say "yes" or "no." Informal gestures and slang that is unclear may lead to confusion in the written record.
3) Your answers need to be audible and verbal. In other words, do not simply nod or shake your head in response to an inquiry. You must say something for the court reporter to transcribe.
4) If there is an objection to a question, you must stop speaking until your lawyer gives you instruction on how to proceed. Do not talk over your attorney.
5) Slow it down. Do not speak too quickly. Be precise in your word choice. Again, someone who fires off words like a machine gun risks creating an inaccurate record of their testimony. Words can be missed.
6) Do not answer any questions that you do not understand, are poorly phrased, too vague, or misuse terms of art. It is not your job to create a sensible question. Ask the attorney to repeat or rephrase the question.

Deposition Strategy

A deposition is a discovery tool. It is something utilized by the opposing counsel in an effort to assess their case, gain advantage, and learn what it is the deponent might say at trial. Their intentions are adverse to yours. They are not your friend and the lawsuit will continue no matter what you say, how well you explain yourself, or how amazing you present. In other words, you are not there to impress anyone but your lawyer. You impress your lawyer by following his instructions to the letter. At the end, there is no applause and the case does not magically disappear. The plaintiff's lawyer will not realize they made a horrible mistake by suing you, apologizing profusely as you graciously accept their prompt dismissal of the case. It just does not work that way. Moreover, even if you do convince them of anything at all, they will not let you know it. At least, not until they are certain there will be no settlement offer, you are not afraid to leave the matter to a jury, and they have virtually zero chance of prevailing.

A deposition is a show. You should assume everything that happens in the deposition to be part of the attorney's strategy. The water I make sure you have is a prop. Use it to ponder a question, buy yourself time to think, and keep your throat moist.

That said, it is also a professional legal proceeding. Typically, I will know the opposing lawyer. I will probably greet them, perhaps shake their hand, and treat them respectfully. These are people I work with often. We have a symbiotic relationship. Do not be offended that I chuckle at their joke or ask about their children. We are advocates. If done right, each respects the other as a worthy adversary and usually treats each other as such. That said, we see each other differently. Each of us believes we are the white knight and the other is on the dark side.

I am often asked if my client must shake the hand of the opposing lawyer. Of course, the answer is "no." But, I must say that it is generally considered to be bad form if they do offer their hand and you refuse it. My suggestion is for you to let your lawyer know beforehand if this is an issue, and they will arrange your entrance in such a way that you will likely avoid the "offer" of an extended hand in the first place.

Mr. Nice Guy

Most, but not all, lawyers will be friendly at first. They will ask you about your background, family, where you were raised, your hobbies, etc. Why? Is it because they care? No. They want you to relax. They want you to engage in a conversation with them. These questions are allowed because the net cast in a discovery deposition is far greater than those allowed at trial. In a deposition, an attorney is allowed to inquire as to facts that are either relevant or likely to lead to the discovery of relevant evidence. So, yes, they can ask those questions, and, no, your lawyer probably cannot interfere with their ability to ask them.

The art of conversation necessarily implies a back and forth; it means there is a free exchange of information without hesitation between you and them, a dialogue. I hate conversations in a deposition, unless I am the one taking the deposition. A conversation means you are not giving your lawyer the opportunity to step in and defend you. I might as well be bound and gagged in a corner. Let your lawyer represent you. Once you answer a question, any objections are waived and your lawyer cannot give you further instruction in regard to the question.

Remember this is not a conversation. You are only in the room because you are involved in a lawsuit, and the law requires your attendance. The person sitting across the table wishes to take from you. They want your time, your sense of security, your reputation, and of course, your money. Do not forget, they are the adversary. At the same time, presenting as a hostile witness is also something to avoid. Remain calm, cool, and collected. Answer the question without getting dragged into an emotional dogfight. You will lose.

Beware, though, that the "nice guy" strategy might change while you follow my instructions. Few attorneys do it well, but there are certainly those few who change up the game plan when things do not go their way by being kind. They might begin "pushing" things a bit by challenging your answers or goading you into giving more information. They might scoff or belittle you. Never mind that strategy because that is *all* it is. Strategy. Nothing more, nothing less. Do not buy into it by letting your ego get the better of you. Take the high road. Show little to no emotion. Stay the course and weather the storm. Your lawyer will be there to bring the attorney back in line by minimizing argumentative questions or behavior. When people get angry, they will generally do one of two things:

clam up or open up. They say things they regret later. The responses are emotional, rather than logical. Remember to remain logical.

Short and Sweet

My goal in defending a deposition is to get it over with as quickly as possible, disclosing the least amount of information and insight into my case strategy as possible. I suppose I should mention, however, that certain states might have rules that require full disclosure. That is, if there are rules limiting a witness to testifying at trial <u>only</u> about information disclosed in the deposition, that "goal" would necessarily change.

That said, my general instruction to my clients is always the same: determine you understand the question, think to yourself what are the fewest possible words you can use to answer the question truthfully, pause for half a second, and then answer. Brevity is key.

Whether we are born this way or trained this way, lawyers "feed" off information. The longer the response, the hungrier we become. We dissect a response until there is nothing left. In the end, the final answer may not resemble the original. For this, lawyers are often accused of "twisting" testimony. But, much of the time, we are doing nothing of the sort. It just works out that way on occasion. Long-winded answers are "punished."

Tips for the Professional

There are two ways I help my medical clients understand this and utilize strategies they have already learned, and I believe this strategy is probably effective for almost any professional deponent. The best technique is to point out that professionals speak to one another in a type of shorthand. They do not explain things to one another that should be commonly understood by most practitioners. They do not have time; they are too busy. Also, to do so might be insulting to their colleague. So, use medical or other professional shorthand when answering questions. Do not explain the test or procedure, its purpose, etc. Speak to the opposing attorney as though they are similarly trained. If they do not understand your answer, they must ask for clarification. Many lawyers do not want to show their lack of understanding and will simply pretend they "get it" and move on to the next question.

For some, you might recall your oral boards. The more information you sought, the harder the questions became. Questions were not met with answers from the examiners; they were met with harder questions. The more they tried to show how skilled they already were, the more the examiners probed. Their faces were devoid of expression or of understanding. The purpose of this was to get the young doctors questioning themselves, their skill, their understanding, and answers.

No Volunteering

Volunteering is the root of all evil. It can take many forms. Intonation, body posture, quizzical looks, questions about the question, and just flat out talking about something that was not asked are all forms of volunteering. This is sometimes hard for many people to overcome, but if educated about certain “techniques” utilized by lawyers during a deposition, you might anticipate and understand your instructions and know when they are straying off the plotted course.

Loaded Terms

Lawyers typically develop a "theme" in their case: You were driving too "fast;" You "overdosed" the patient; You were "rushing around" and did not watch what you were doing; You were "overworked" or "tired" or "angry" when you did something; Perhaps you "overlooked" a "red flag" or "dangerous sign" that led to serious injury.

Because of this, many lawyers might try enlisting you to perpetuate their own theme by having you "endorse" and "accept" their characterization of the events at issue. They do so by selecting one or two choice words and injecting them into their own question. Once you answer the question affirmatively, they repeat and repeat the word throughout the course of the proceeding.

Example

Attorney: My client had enlarged lymph nodes, didn't he?
Witness: Yes.

Attorney: Doctor, don't you agree that Stage 3 lung cancer is a deadly disease?
Witness: Of course.
Attorney: You also agree, don't you, that enlarged lymph nodes are a "red flag" when it comes to cancer diagnosis, including lung cancer?
Witness: They certainly can be.
Attorney: My client had enlarged lymph nodes, didn't he?
Witness: Yes.
Attorney: How many times did my client present to you with this "red flag" for this deadly disease, and what did you do in the face of that "red flag"?
Witness: [Does the answer really matter at this point?]

Fast-forward to Opening Statement (Argument) at Trial

Attorney: "Members of the jury, the evidence in this case is very straightforward. Dr. Jones wholeheartedly admitted in his own deposition that, despite the fact that my client presented on multiple occasions with a "red flag" for a deadly form of cancer, he did nothing. Instead, he treated him for a cold. Now, my client is dying."

The Corrected Responses

Attorney: Doctor, don't you agree that Stage 3 lung cancer is a deadly disease?
Witness: The prognosis is relatively poor, but it is treatable.
Attorney: Would you agree that enlarged lymph nodes are a "red flag" when it comes to cancer diagnosis, including lung cancer?
Witness: Enlarged lymph nodes are generally a non-specific sign of systemic infection. I would not consider them a "red flag" for cancer, if that is what you are getting at. I cannot generalize like that.

In short, do not let the deposing attorney select your word choices. Although a short answer is preferred when possible, do not sacrifice your case for the sake of brevity. The results could be disastrous. Be patient and selective with what words you are willing to accept or endorse when offered by the deposing lawyer.

Blame the Other Guy

If you are a named defendant, it may be enticing to deflect blame from yourself onto another. In fact, some plaintiffs' attorneys might even purposefully present opportunities for you to cast blame on other defendants. They may seem to console you for having to be involved in the case. “It's all the other guy's fault, isn't it?” “Such a shame you have to be involved, because I'm almost certain you are here because of the other defendant.”

This act is typically a sham. They will employ the same strategy with your co-defendants in their deposition. In the end, you will both blame each other, and the plaintiff's lawyer can simply sit back and watch the fireworks.

Before throwing stones at your co-defendants, talk to your lawyer about whether that would really be an effective strategy in your case. Chances are, you are better off sticking with the facts, not your opinion about what you think someone else did or should have done.

Awkward Silence

Many people have a problem with silence in conversation. It is the way society has programmed us. But, remember that a deposition is not a conversation. Some lawyers may use silence as a tool to draw the witness out. As mentioned previously, volunteering is the root of all evil in a deposition. Do not fall victim to the awkward silence ploy. This may be more easily said than done, if you happen to be a natural "chatterbox." Remember that it is not your job to keep the questions coming. Just wait patiently for the next question, answer it, and then move on.

Memory Challenges

Some deponents prefer to wrap themselves in the temporary comfort of a memory lapse. “I don't recall” seems like such a wonderful escape at the time. However, it can also be very damaging in that it robs you of your own credibility.

For instance, if you have no memory of the events at issue, and the opposing party does, then guess who wins? Not you.

There have been occasions where I have counted the number of “I don't remembers” in a deposition, and then challenged the witness with it at trial. “It is interesting Ms. X that you have such a detailed recollection of the events for our jury when your lawyer asks you the questions, but do you know how many times you told me you did not remember the events during your deposition six months ago?"

Obviously, there will be times when "I don't remember" is the only answer you can give. But, do not overuse this fallback. If the supposition behind the question is absurd, you might consider answering: "I do not recall anything like that occurring, and I certainly would if it happened that way." Another possibility might be: "If that event would have happened that way, I definitely would have (fill in the blank)."

Refreshing Recollection

Most states allow counsel to ask you to reveal and discuss with them any documents you reviewed to prepare for your deposition to the extent those documents "refreshed your recollection" of the events at issue. This is based largely upon a federal rule of evidence that has been codified in most state court jurisdictions.

However, this rule does not allow counsel to invade any privileges that might apply, including the attorney-client or husband-wife privilege. Before reciting the list of documents and things you reviewed before your deposition, make sure that the list does not include any privileged communications, including status letters from your attorney or other such documents that would likely fall under a privilege.

Be warned, not all attorneys understand the limitations of the "refreshing recollection" rule and they will argue incessantly that they are entitled to review all documents, privileged or not. For that matter, your own lawyer may not grasp the rule, either. For this reason, discuss with your lawyer, in advance, what documents are subject to disclosure under the rules, should this question arise during your deposition.

Do Not Guess

If you do not know the answer to a question, do not guess or speculate. This cannot be stressed enough. If a question calls for information outside the scope of your expertise, do not let the deposing lawyer draw you outside of your own comfort zone. If you find yourself providing a definitive response about what happened at a certain time, but you were not even present, there is a problem.

There will obviously be times where events likely occurred a certain way because that is the way they always happen, but a deposition is not the time to make these assumptions. Remember, since there is a lawsuit pending, things may not have unfolded in their typical way this time. Focus on what you know, what you saw, what you said, and what you felt. Other witnesses can and will do the same for themselves.

Changing Your Answer

Yes, you may change or expand upon your answers in the deposition. However, before doing so, take a break with your lawyer to discuss any developing realizations and impulses you might have to distrust your previous testimony. It is not uncommon for witnesses to second guess themselves about the facts as they begin thinking about the incident details during a deposition. Memories can be triggered by subsequent answers.

Do Not Try to Be Clever

No amount of bad TV lawyer shows will bestow upon you the power to frighten a tenacious lawyer away from asking you more detailed questions. For that matter, sarcasm does not make good reading and can, in fact, lead to false testimony when read back outside of the context of the deposition setting. Do not try to be clever, cocky, argumentative, sarcastic or cunning. In all likelihood, this will simply lengthen your deposition and lead to factual inconsistencies when attempting to interpret your testimony at trial.

Fantastic examples demonstrating how this tactic can completely backfire and damage your case are the Justin Bieber deposition videos. I would submit that you will have a difficult time identifying anyone who found Mr. Bieber's presentation compelling. He did nothing but weaken his case, and I would be willing to wager that the deposing attorney was secretly smiling to himself on the inside as he calculated the case value rising with each passing moment.

You should understand that a deposition, when printed, does not read like a novel. There are no descriptions, explanations or other details contained within the pages that will assist the reader with context or mood. Having your attorney show you what a printed deposition looks like will give you some perspective in this regard. Consider asking if your attorney has depositions from other similar cases the opposing attorney has taken. This might improve your pre deposition confidence and give you a preview of things to come.

Anticipating Questions

Do not anticipate questions. When you do this, it means you are not thinking and pausing before your answer. You are also preventing your lawyer from objecting, if necessary. Firing out an answer before the question is finished breaks many of the deposition rules set out above.

Authoritative Texts

An "authoritative text" is any writing given a special evidentiary designation in the law. If you are asked to identify any texts or journals you consider to be "authoritative," do not answer the question. It is loaded and requires you to provide a legal opinion. In essence, you will be testifying that all information contained within those writings is true, accurate, and reflective of the "standard of care."

Appropriate questions about writings might center around what texts or periodicals you find "helpful," but not authoritative. Some writings might even be "generally relied upon" in your trade or profession. But, do not feel compelled to endorse everything contained within such materials by agreeing they are "authoritative." This would be a mistake, unless your attorney has a special advance strategy in mind and instructs you otherwise.

Take a Break

Try to take a break every sixty to ninety minutes, depending upon the anticipated length of a deposition. Depositions are stressful, emotionally demanding proceedings, and even a short five or ten-minute break will likely rejuvenate your brain and allow you to re-center yourself.

If you are a smoker, take a smoke break. The last thing your attorney wants is a client going through a nicotine fit during their deposition.

Consulting with Your Lawyer

You are always entitled to consult with your lawyer privately. However, the rules require the witness to answer the pending question before doing so.

If you begin anticipating upcoming questions based upon information not previously discussed with your lawyer, call for a quick break and discuss the issue with them. Strategizing on the spur of the moment is better than listening to new, undisclosed information for the first time while your client is testifying in the deposition.

Just a Few More Questions

Although generally an honest miscalculation by the deposing lawyer, never believe it when you are assured there are only "a few more questions." This is sometimes a ploy aimed at encouraging you to let your guard down or "hurry through" the last few remaining (but critical) questions. Ignore the suggestion and proceed as though the deposition will likely go on longer than promised.

Power Play

There is a difference in my profession between a trial lawyer and a litigator. A litigator is a lawyer who prepares for trial while focusing on strategizing a settlement or other case resolution, expecting the case will never make it before a jury. As a result, they rarely try cases. On the other hand, a trial lawyer is someone who handles the case from start to finish with the expectation that the matter will be tried before a jury, but accepting that the best strategy may be settlement or successful motion practice. As a result, trial lawyers are in court far more frequently, and that is the way we like it.

Trial attorneys are typically aggressive, self-assured and sometimes arrogant people. We thrive in conflict. For this reason, it is not uncommon for opposing lawyers to "lock horns" and "push the envelope" with one another during a deposition. Harsh words may be exchanged and temperatures in the room will rise. But, the vast majority of the time, there will either be a stalemate or one attorney will maintain dominance over the other. You will typically discover at this time whether you are being represented by a litigator or a trial lawyer.

Objections

Objections during a deposition are limited, in general, to "the form of the question." As there is no judge in the room, this is the universal way lawyers preserve an objection to the question being asked, so the judge can rule on the issue later. Unless your lawyer instructs you "not to answer the question," the rules require you to answer the question pending.

Lawyers are not allowed to "coach" their witnesses by specifying the nature of their objection, as we are required to do at trial. For instance, if I were to object on the basis of "speculation," my client would likely reply that they "cannot speculate" about the answer. This would likely be considered coaching.

But, if your lawyer is objecting, they are telling you there is a problem with the question. So, if you did not catch it the first time, listen to the question again and proceed with caution.

The most common reasons for "objections to form" are: (1) the question is compound; (2) the question assumes incorrect facts about prior testimony or other events that are in dispute; (3) the question contains a long, unwieldy preamble that is simply confusing or incorrect; (4) the question is unfair in that it assumes there is only an "either/or" response available, when there may be a middle ground; (5) the question asks the witness to speculate or guess.

Keep this list in mind when you hear your attorney object during the deposition. Also remember that "irrelevant" is not typically an appropriate discovery objection, as long as the information sought might lead to the discovery of relevant evidence.

Compound Questions

Compound questions can take two primary forms. They may either be multi-part or multi-faceted questions calling for multiple answers, simultaneously. Or, they may be a deceptive single-part question that assumes an untrue fact somewhere within the body of the question.

An example of the latter type is: "Did you apply your brakes before or after you ran the red light?" In this respect, there are different ways one might approach the question. The witness could reject the question outright and refuse to answer based upon the way the question is phrased. On the other hand, the witness could appropriately reject the question in part and answer with a compound response as follows: "First, I did not run the red light, but I did apply my brakes before the intersection."

The former method tends to work best with inexperienced witnesses, and is the safest method. On the other hand, if the witness is comfortable with providing a compound answer, I will usually allow my clients to proceed in this fashion to the extent it might hasten the proceeding.

Videotaped Depositions

It is common practice in high value cases to videotape depositions. Your "Notice of Deposition" is required to specify whether your deposition will be videotaped. Make sure you ask your lawyer about this during your pre-deposition preparation conference.

My practice is to videotape all depositions, with very limited and strategic exceptions. The reason for this is probably obvious. I plan on taking all cases to trial. There is nothing like a videotape to highlight key testimony for the jury. Awkward pauses, stutters, deceptive eye movements, uncomfortable body posturing, sarcasm, arrogance and other aspects of a witness' demeanor are all caught on tape and preserved for the jury. Videotape is an essential trial tool that has become much easier to utilize effectively. It is far more effective than reading a deposition excerpt to the jury during trial.

While the tape is rolling, remember that your video may be played back for the jury. Dress and behave appropriately. Although some lawyers may disagree with me, I believe the witness should always address the lawyer asking the questions, not the camera. The camera is a distraction, and my clients cannot afford to be distracted while providing sworn testimony. Neither can you.

Perpetuated Depositions

A perpetuated deposition may be taken when witnesses will be unavailable for trial. The procedural rules allow the lawyers to videotape depositions of anticipated witnesses and play them back for the jury at trial. The procedure is different than a discovery deposition, since the scope of those depositions is limited by the evidentiary rules applicable at trial. Specific objections are raised by the attorneys, and there will be cross-examination and re-direct examination of the witness at the time of recording.

Deposition Testimony Checklist

1. Dress nicely and act appropriately.
2. Listen carefully to the question and your lawyer's instructions.
3. If you do not understand the question or it misstates prior testimony, do not answer it.
4. Do not ask a question about a confusing question. Do not answer it.
5. Pause before answering the question.
6. Be brief and truthful in your answer.
7. Answer only the question asked. Do not volunteer.
8. Do not "take the lawyer on" with your wit or knowledge. You will lose.
9. Do not engage the lawyer in conversation.
10. Do not argue your case. You will lose.
11. Above all, consider your answer carefully.

9

Routine Litigation Detours

Trial Scheduling and Set-Overs

The first thing to understand about a civil trial is that civil trials are always considered less important than criminal trials. This is because, in our country, all criminals have a right to a speedy trial. Therefore, if the criminal trial docket is busy, civil trials take a backseat and must wait their turn to have a trial judge appointed. Different jurisdictions handle the appointment of trial judges differently. Each jurisdiction has developed its own method of assigning trial judges so that it, hopefully, expedites the process and makes it less likely that your trial date will be set over or moved for some other reason.

That said, it is typical for an initial trial setting to be moved by one or more of the parties, or the court. Trial dates are set by the court; I am convinced, in an effort to simply move the case along. If there is a date set for trial, the parties and lawyers are more likely to keep the case active and the discovery process ongoing. In other words, the case is less likely to wallow around in a quagmire for any lengthy period.

That said, different courts and different jurisdictions have longer or shorter trial dockets, and your lawyer will have a better idea of how long your case might take before it gets to trial. Also, depending on the complexity of the case, trial dates can also be moved to accommodate witnesses. If there is a significant of number of witnesses, it becomes harder to coordinate a trial date to accommodate everyone's schedule. Additionally, not only are witnesses a problem, but trial lawyers are also difficult to schedule with, if there are more than two or three lawyers working on any given case.

Some trial dockets take as little as six months, others take as long as three to six years. It simply depends upon the type of case you have, the complexity, the number of criminal cases in front of your civil case, and any number of variables that might occur or demand attention. As time passes, witnesses disappear, move, die, and forget. These are all factors that go into a trial lawyer's strategy and analysis.

As you learn of upcoming dates, it is probably worthwhile to discuss the dates with your lawyer. Some dates will be "firm dates," others will not. If you are planning a vacation or other family event where you will be unavailable, you should make sure your lawyer knows about those dates ahead of time. This will circumvent a great deal of scheduling problems as the trial date draws near.

Alternative Dispute Resolution

Alternative dispute resolution (ADR) is something that most courts require litigants to participate in prior to either obtaining a trial date or making it to trial. The lawyers on each side must certify that they have engaged in "good faith efforts" in an attempt to resolve the case, short of trial. This typically involves a court settlement conference, mediation, or arbitration. These rules developed simply because many cases were making it all the way to trial and judges were learning that the parties never even attempted to work out a settlement or compromise.

Depending upon the type of case, you may or may not be involved in the ADR process. If you are a defendant and the case is meritless, it is likely that you would be involved in some type of ADR. Also, if you are an insured defendant, and you have signed a consent form authorizing settlement, it is unlikely that you would participate in the ADR process. Most of the time, the insurance representative will attend and has a certain amount of "authority" in which to settle the case. In other words, the insurance representative or claims specialist will have a certain amount of money they have been authorized to spend to resolve the case by way of settlement.

10

Strategies for Case Resolution

Cases resolve in several ways. They can be settled, dismissed by the plaintiff, thrown out by the court on a motion for summary judgment or other "dispositive motion," or resolved in some sort of a trial or arbitration proceeding. Not every type of resolution method is available in every case. For the most part, cases are settled, dismissed, or tried.

To determine whether the case should be settled, at least from the defense standpoint, a significant number of considerations are at play. The trial lawyer will need to determine the strength of the case by analyzing the evidence and the witnesses available. The court, judge, prospective jury pool, and skill of opposing counsel are also due considerations.

It is not uncommon for cases to be filed and later dismissed by the plaintiff litigants. As discovery goes on, money can run out or emotions can die down, evidence can be destroyed, key witnesses can pass away, and/or life circumstances can change. What was once considered a strong case by the plaintiff's trial attorney may all of a sudden fall flat on its face and become one that is simply not worth the risk of trial.

On the other hand, as the litigation process continues, both sides may realize that there are risks of trial that support a settlement strategy. There are various ways to go about settling a case, some of them more popular than others. Each involves strategy in its own right.

Whatever the case may be, after the majority of the discovery process is complete, your trial attorney should have a good idea of where the case is headed. The chances of prevailing are probably more obvious than they were initially. There is always risk and absolutely no guarantee that either side will prevail when it comes to jury trials. To "compromise," there are a number of ways a settlement can be reached.

Direct Attorney Negotiation

It is typically my practice to attempt settlement by negotiating directly with the opposing lawyer. A demand is made by the plaintiff's attorney, essentially arguing the case in its best light, asking for, typically, more than the attorney believes the case is actually worth. Then, after some back and forth about the case and various strategies available, recent jury verdicts, the latest judicial rulings, etc., the parties go back and forth and ultimately reach a resolution of the case.

However, in recent years, other avenues of settlement have been created. Many insurance companies simply prefer having a third party make determinations about settlement.

Mediations

Mediation is a process held outside of the court. Attorneys on all sides will work with one another in selecting the appropriate mediator or mediators for any given case. Mediators are not typically appointed by the court. Instead, they are often retired judges or respected lawyers who are able to successfully play the "middle ground" in helping the parties come to a mutual understanding about the case value. Typically, these mediation sessions are held outside of the courthouse in conference rooms located within one of the attorneys' offices.

Strategies for mediation can vary significantly. However, in most situations, attorneys will provide the mediator with their perspective on the case in a confidential way. The mediator will review some of the key evidence and statements, meet with witnesses, if available, watch video, or engage any number of techniques that might help them analyze a "mediated case value." Oftentimes, the involvement of a disinterested third party who is employed to provide an objective opinion helps the parties come to a mutual understanding about settlement. The costs of the mediator are split between all parties. The mediator then meets privately with each party and develops a strategy for settlement. Whatever the case may be, with any luck, a skilled mediator will be able to "take in the room," and weigh the various personalities at play, as well as the facts and circumstances of any given case to determine whether a case is likely to settle or not.

The process may take less than one day or it may drag on for weeks. After the parties leave the office for the day, phone calls and e-mails may be exchanged in further efforts to reach a case resolution. Most cases that go to mediation, however, resolve either the day of mediation or within a week or two following the mediation, if at all.

Not every case that goes to mediation will resolve. One thing a mediation will allow the parties to do, however, is to come to an understanding that the case must simply be tried to a jury. It could be that the case valuation is simply so far apart on each side that compromise is not possible short of a jury trial.

Mediators have different techniques and tactics they use to settle cases. A great deal of the process, however, involves simply listening to each side and making a determination as to whether or not the case is one that should be settled. That said, some cases are simply meant to go to trial.

Arbitration

Arbitration is different from mediation. Some cases must be mandatorily arbitrated, others can be voluntarily arbitrated. Arbitrations can be required in some contracts. Additionally, some courts require that all civil cases that do not exceed a certain dollar amount (typically $50,000 to $75,000) must be first arbitrated before a trial will be scheduled.

Arbitrations can be composed of a panel of arbitrators or a single arbitrator. Various courts in a variety of jurisdictions have promulgated rules and guidelines associated with the selection of an arbitration panel or individual arbitrator. However, in almost every case, the parties will have a say in who is selected as an arbitrator or a member of the arbitration panel.

An arbitration is conducted similar to a trial. The primary difference is that there is no judge and jury. Instead, there is an arbitrator or panel of arbitrators hearing all of the evidence. Additionally, arbitrations tend to be far less formal than a trial and Rules of Evidence are not as strictly enforced. Arbitrators are typically lawyers or judges who are paid by each side to listen to the case and make a determination.

Arbitrations are not typically held in a courthouse. They are more likely to occur in a conference room at an office. Each side is entitled to be present to offer evidence and witnesses in support of their case.

Because of the informality associated with arbitrations, they typically run much shorter than trials. In most instances, arbitrations will be substantially shorter in duration than any given trial. Arbitrators are authorized to make decisions about the law and the evidence in every given case.

Once the arbitrator has heard all of the evidence, they will issue a number of findings and conclusions. If appropriate, they will also prepare an award, which is similar to a jury verdict. Depending on the purpose behind the arbitration, the arbitration will be either binding or non-binding.

In the case of a non-binding arbitration, either party reserves the right to appeal the arbitrator's decision and proceed directly to a jury trial. In most cases, there are arbitration rules in every given jurisdiction that provide for a penalty in the event that the appealing party does not improve their chances at trial. In other words, if they receive the same or less advantageous verdict than they received from the arbitrator, there may be costs imposed and, in some cases, attorney's fees can be collected.

In the case of binding arbitration, the arbitrator's decision is not susceptible to challenge. Each party has contractually obligated themselves to comply with the arbitrator's formal decision and award. There is no appeals process and the award will be entered as a matter of law as a judgment in favor of one party or the other. Most cases that require mandatory arbitrations, typically those cases that involve a less substantial amount of money and controversy, will be appealable.

Settlement Conference

Settlement conferences are required in some jurisdictions. In some cases, they can be effective in helping the parties reach resolution. As far as a settlement conference is concerned, some courts appoint certain judges to serve as the settlement conference judge.

The judge, essentially, serves as a mediator in the case and attempts to help the parties reach case resolution. This type of settlement technique can be effective in cases where the amount in controversy is minimal or the type of dispute is one that can be remedied quickly with a judge's input. However, complex cases that involve substantial damages are unlikely to be settled in a mandatory settlement conference presided over by a judge. That is not to say that they never work in those situations. However, judges typically do not have the ability to preside over a settlement conference for half a day or longer to reach resolution. If the issues are straightforward and the damages minimal, these cases are more likely to be resolved within an hour or two of the judge having contact with all parties.

11

Trial

If you have made it through the discovery process and completed your probable mandatory ADR proceeding without resolution, your next step may be trial. By then, your trial date will probably have been pushed back on at least two or three occasions, maybe more. Your deposition will be complete, and you will know who the witnesses are for and against you. Key documents and other exhibits will be known by all, and it will be time for you to walk up the steps to the courthouse.

In all likelihood, you will have met with your trial lawyer and spoken on the phone or e-mailed on many occasions getting the case ready for trial. Your lawyer has probably had an opportunity to show you various trial exhibits he or she intends to use and have you weigh in on their effectiveness. You should have read your deposition by now at least three to four times and have it memorized. For that matter, you probably should have read all of the witnesses' testimony in the case and have a good idea what they intend to say about you and/or the matter.

In other words, there should be no huge surprises by the time you sit down in the courtroom with your lawyer armed for trial. Of course, I did use the word "should." This is because there are always surprises at trial. Some of them are simply smaller than others.

What follows is a general summary of what steps you can expect to witness during the trial process. With any luck, you feel comfortable enough in your case so that you will not feel like a "fish out of water." Nevertheless, there will be times where you are frightened, nervous, angry, thrilled, or any number of human emotions that can be described. Whoever said that the circus was the greatest show on earth had never been to trial.

Witness Chair Checklist

There are a number of "constants" that seem to prevail when preparing for witness testimony. The key to remember is that not all jurors think alike. Not all jurors like the things that you like. Juries want to relate to you. Keep in mind that the slightest detail can turn the jury either against you or in your favor. You want to be seen as a friendly, honest, modest, and likable person. Eliminate all possible character reflections from your physical presence. For instance, some people simply do not trust people with facial hair. Why risk having it? It grows back. Some people do not like smokers. So, chew Nicorette.

Before you make it to the courtroom, get a good night's sleep and eat a healthy breakfast. Avoid too much coffee and watch the medications. Drive carefully to and from the courthouse and be a courteous driver. You never know whether there is a juror watching you.

If you drive an expensive car, park far from the courthouse and walk. Do not park illegally or jaywalk. Follow the letter of the law!

In the courthouse, do not talk about the case or comment on witnesses. Do not be loud or offensive.

You might think this is too much, but you need to be as inoffensive as possible. Case in point: wash your hands after using the restroom! Please do not gross out our jurors. When I say pay attention to the details, that is exactly what I mean. Do not give the jury *any* reason whatsoever to dislike you to the extent you can possibly help it. This is much easier said than done.

That said, these are the basics:

1. Your dress should be as discussed with your lawyer. Conservative and professional is the best plan. No flashy jewelry or watches. No body piercings. Men should shave. Tattoos should be covered. Go easy on the makeup. Consider the jury you have selected when selecting your outfits for the next day. Do not smoke between breaks.

2. Do not slouch. Slide your buttocks as far back in the chair as possible. Pull your chair in and keep your hands folded comfortably on the table in front of you both as a witness and as a party at counsel table.
3. When on the stand, listen to the questions carefully and look at the individual asking you questions directly. Be advised, ***either*** lawyer can call you as a witness in the case whenever they wish. Be prepared for this. You might be the first witness called!
4. Do not respond if there has been an objection made. Wait for the judge to rule, in the event of an objection. A "sustained" objection means you will not answer the question as it was posed. An "overruled" objection means that you should go ahead and answer the question.
5. As you begin to answer the question, turn your head and address the jury. Speak to the jury in answering the question. Avoid slang and informal or offensive language. They are the ones weighing your fate.
6. Answer the question directly. Explain your answer, if necessary. Do not be rude, sarcastic, or confrontational in your response. Avoid evasive answers and signal your attorney by commenting that your answer is incomplete, in the event you are cut off.
7. Do not look at your lawyer during cross-examination by opposing counsel and do not talk to the judge unless spoken to. If your lawyer has an objection, she will make it. You do not want to appear as though you have anything to hide or that you are your lawyer's puppet.
8. While listening to witnesses, do not make faces, comments, or sounds of disgruntlement. Be respectful, even if you disagree with the statements being made. It is up to your lawyer to challenge the credibility of the testimony being heard.

Anatomy of a Trial

Pretrial Motions

Your lawyer will be arguing what are commonly referred to as pretrial motions. Pretrial motions are general discussions and argument about the evidence that each side expects the other will present at trial. Sometimes, these are referred to as "motions *in limine*." This generally means that your lawyer is asking the court to limit certain evidence or prevent it from coming in altogether.

Many motions in *limine* filed by experienced trial attorneys are simply agreed on prior to argument. Others have to be hashed out. Most lawyers have a standard set of motions they intend to file that will set out the general principles that all parties can agree to concerning the way evidence will be disclosed at trial. However, in most cases, there are two or three key issues that your lawyer will be focusing on that could make a substantial difference in the way evidence is delivered to the jury.

Regardless, your lawyer will be able to give you an update once the judge has made his or her determinations about the motions. Some evidentiary determinations will be unexpected, for better or for worse. As mentioned in previous chapters, some judges simply make up the rules as they go along, even though their opinions may be completely unsupported in the law. A trial lawyer needs to be prepared for anything.

Jury Selection

When it is time for jury selection, approximately thirty to fifty people will file into the courtroom and sit down on the back benches. They will be placed in a certain order and the judge will ask them a number of questions to determine whether they are able to sit as jurors at the trial.

Jurors come in all shapes and sizes with all levels of education. It is the lawyer's job during the "*voir dire*" process to determine whether any particular jurors should be specifically excluded. Most of the time, there will be a hodgepodge of good and bad jurors sitting in judgment on your case. The fact is, your lawyer does not have the ability to eliminate everyone he or she does not like. There are only a limited number of "challenges" that your lawyer will have (typically three) to exercise in eliminating jurors.

There are, however, an unlimited number of challenges "for cause," that can be issued by the court. One of the objectives of your trial lawyer will be to ferret out the bad jurors and which of those bad jurors can be excused "for cause." Perhaps they are too biased or have personal experience or knowledge of some of the parties or witnesses. Whatever the case may be, it is up to the trial lawyer to ferret out any potential issues that might arise in the event a certain prospective juror makes it on the panel.

The process of selecting a jury can take anywhere from half a day to a few weeks. However, in the vast majority of cases, judges simply will not put up with a *voir dire* process that takes longer than a full day.

You should note that, depending on the size of your jury and the estimated length of trial, the judge will also permit the selection of one to three "alternate jurors" to serve in the case. Alternates will become a sitting juror in the event another juror is excused for some unforeseen reason. The longer the trial, the more likely one or more jurors will be lost due to illness, death, imprisonment, family emergency, or inappropriate conduct. I have had one juror excused for sleeping during the trial.

Opening Statements

After the jury is selected, they will be sworn in by the judge and the lawyers will be allowed to present their opening statements. There are various rules associated with opening statements and how they are presented. Whatever the case may be, however, most lawyers will present an opening statement explaining to the jury what evidence they can expect to see and what that evidence will show. Although some lawyers refer to opening statement as "opening argument," lawyers are generally not allowed to *argue* the evidence. Instead, they must present it in a way that is objectively reasonable. Arguments are reserved for the end of trial, not the beginning. Nevertheless, a good trial lawyer will figure out a way to present the case as an advocate and in the light most favorable to his or her client. Opening statements vary in length depending upon the number of issues being presented and the amount of evidence the jury will be asked to consider and go through.

Plaintiff's Case-in-Chief

After legal argument, jury selection, and opening statements, the plaintiff has his or her opportunity to present their side of the case first. Witnesses will be presented, evidence will be offered, and the case will begin to unfold pursuant to the plaintiff's lawyer's timing and discretion, for the most part.

It will be at this time that most defendants feel defeated. However, I often have to remind my clients that we have not had an opportunity to present our evidence. A trial rarely involves a constant flow of favorable evidence to one specific side. Instead, it is more of an ebb and flow that litigants experience. There will be good days and bad days. Some witnesses will present favorably and others will not. The course of trial will flow on, but it will be almost impossible to tell which way your jury is leaning.

Once all of plaintiff's witnesses have testified and all evidence has been marked and entered in the plaintiff's case, the plaintiff's attorney will "rest." At that time, the defense lawyer will need to preserve any issues for appeal by arguing a "motion for directed verdict."

At that time, the defense lawyer will argue to the court why the plaintiff has not sustained their burden of proof and the court should enter judgment and take the matter from the jury entirely. Although it is extremely rare, motions for directed verdict do occur. Typically, motions are granted because the plaintiff, despite having produced all of their evidence, simply fails to meet their burden of proof in regard to one of the essential elements of their claim. If this happens, the judgment is entered in defendant's favor and the case is terminated. The jury is sent home without rendering a verdict.

Defendant's Case-in-Chief

If the court determines that a motion for directed verdict is unsupported, it will allow the case to continue. At that point, it is the defense lawyer's opportunity to present his or her own case. The same process will be followed in which witnesses are brought and evidence is admitted.

Once the defense lawyer has presented all witnesses and introduced all evidence, the case is still not over.

Plaintiff's Rebuttal

Because plaintiff has the burden of proof, they get one last bite at the apple. At the end of the defendant's case, the plaintiff can also move for a directed verdict. The defense could move for a directed verdict again, but these motions rarely go anywhere. Whatever the case may be, the plaintiff will be able to present rebuttal witnesses.

Rebuttal witnesses are witnesses who are allowed to testify about the defense case in the event that the issues raised by the defense were not completely covered in plaintiff's case-in-chief. Now, it should be made perfectly clear that most rebuttal witnesses are actually witnesses that could have or did present testimony during the plaintiff's original case-in-chief. Nevertheless, no good trial lawyer would fail to take advantage of the opportunity to present his or her witnesses again. Usually, a plaintiff's attorney will be allowed to "rehash" at least some of the arguments before the defense attorney can appropriately prohibit this from occurring by objecting.

Regardless, plaintiff's rebuttal is generally limited in duration and does not go on for much longer than a day or two. Most of the time, it is over within a matter of hours.

Final Arguments

After plaintiff rests again, following their rebuttal, the court will hear additional arguments and the jury instructions will be promulgated. Jury instructions will generally be argued over a period of days. They are an essential piece of any trial lawyer's case and are often used during closing arguments. The uniform jury instructions are available in most courts. They are a series of instructions that have been tested and tried over the years and most judges will not deviate from a uniform jury instruction. That said, there are a number of issues that might come up in any given case that require special attention. In those cases, your trial attorney will craft a "special instruction" that he or she wants read to the jury. Of course, like most special instructions, the opposing attorney will generally disagree with the way they are crafted. The back and forth that goes on in arguing about the jury instructions is probably one of the most important aspects of the case. These instructions determine how the jury will compare the facts and evidence to the law in your case.

Closing Arguments

Once the court has been assured that all evidence has been admitted and marked, the jury instructions have been determined by the court, and a verdict form has been created and approved, the parties will move on to closing arguments. For the most part, most people probably know what a closing argument is about. It is the quintessential conceptualization of what it is to be a trial lawyer. It is at that point that the trial lawyer argues their case to the jury and compares the facts and evidence to the law.

The reality is that, no matter how powerful one's closing argument might be, the jurors have most likely already made up their mind. The best thing you can hope for as a trial attorney is that you have made a strong case before presenting your closing argument and that you can effectively tie your evidence to the points of law the judge will be asking them to consider in deliberating on the case.

Once the attorneys have completed their closing arguments, and the plaintiff has an opportunity to argue a rebuttal closing argument, the jury will be read the instructions by the court. The court will go through each and every one of the instructions for the jury and provide them with a copy. The judge will also read through the verdict form and explain how the form is to be filled out. Thereafter, the jury will be retired to deliberate.

Jury Deliberation

Jury deliberations are one of the most nerve-racking events one could possibly sit through. Every minute seems like an hour. Every hour seems like an eternity. The second-guessing that occurs is ridiculous. Nevertheless, there is nothing that can be done.

Some judges will take questions from the jury that are written out. It will be the judge's obligation to read those questions to all lawyers and determine whether it is something that can be answered without interfering with the deliberation process. Some jurors may ask no questions, some may ask dozens. Regardless, one thing can be certain, there is almost no way of knowing exactly what the jury is thinking and why they are thinking it. It is definitely a time you will feel helpless.

As a trial lawyer, the only solace I get is feeling as though I did everything I possibly could to win the case. If I failed, then there was nothing I could have done to prevent it. As long as I have that feeling, I am fairly confident that the outcome will be fair and reasonable. Of course, this is of little to no consolation to my clients. Nevertheless, I believe that they often feel the same way.

The Verdict

Once the jury has deliberated and reached its determinations, they will summon the bailiff. The bailiff will then notify the judge that the jury has reached a verdict. It will be either the judge's clerk or the bailiff who contacts the trial lawyers and lets them know that a verdict has been returned. After receiving this notice, the parties are to return to the courtroom and await the jury's determination.

The lawyers and their clients will sit at counsel table and wait in silence for the jury to return. Once the jury returns the verdict, the judge will ask the jurors if they have reached a determination. If the answer is "yes," the judge will collect the verdict and review it.

In some jurisdictions, the judge will return the verdict to the jury foreperson and have the jury foreperson read the verdict. In other cases, the judge may simply read the verdict out loud.

Whatever the case may be, it is considered improper courtroom etiquette for the parties to acknowledge in some sense the verdict that was determined. There should be no outbursts, clapping, crying, or screaming. Instead, I always instruct my clients to remain seated and silent until I can explain what happened and what the jury ultimately determined.

The jury is then thanked for their time and dismissed. The case is over. You will have either won or lost. There are typically no "ties" in the courtroom, unless there has been a mistrial or the jury could not come to agreement.

Regardless of whether you have won or lost your case, there will be appeal issues that need to be considered. Most of the time, appellate issues do not come up. There are a limited number of reasons that jury verdicts can be appealed. Additionally, to have a successful appeal, the evidentiary or other issue on appeal must be substantial. Your lawyer will be able to provide you with an evaluation of whether or not you can expect an appeal or whether, if you lost, you should appeal.

In most situations, trial lawyers will not actually file an appeal, themselves. Instead, there are skilled appellate lawyers who will handle that aspect of the case.

In the vast majority of cases that are tried to a jury, the case is never appealed. There may be subsequent negotiations that occur after a verdict has been entered to avoid an appeal and to settle the case, but only a handful of verdicts will ever make it to the appellate court.

12

Frequently Asked Questions

Q: Can I be sued even though I did nothing wrong?

A: Yes. Anyone can pay a filing fee and file a lawsuit in court. You do not have to be a lawyer and you do not even have to have a legitimate case.

Q: Why do judges allow frivolous lawsuits to go on?

A: Oftentimes, it is not up to the judge. Judges can decide issues of law. However, where facts are in dispute, a jury must decide whose version of the facts is correct. The judge cannot take away factual issues from the jury, unless no reasonable person could see things differently.

Q: How can I prevent a frivolous lawsuit from being filed against me?

A: You cannot. You can be sued by anyone, at any time, for anything. You can only document what has happened and preserve evidence when you believe a lawsuit might arise from actions you take.

Q: Are there remedies for frivolous lawsuits?

A: Yes. Most states have statutes that allow wrongfully sued defendants to file suit for attorney fees they incurred because of the meritless claim. I will often include a counter-claim in my Answer in such instances seeking attorney fee reimbursement.

Q: Should I represent myself or hire a lawyer?

A: Under very limited circumstances, you do not need an attorney. But, if this is preferable, the lawyer you consult with will tell you so and send you on the right path.

Q: Can I recover damages for the stress that litigation caused me?

A: Not typically. There are claims for intentional infliction of emotional distress, however, which may be brought. There is a very high level of proof and emotional injury required to sustain such a claim.

Q: The complaint or answer is full of lies. Is that defamation?

A: No. Statements made in a legal pleading or petition are privileged and do not subject anyone to civil liability. A press release about the lawsuit, however, must be carefully worded to avoid civil liability for defamation.

Q: Can I sue the lawyer who sued me?

A: Probably not. Lawyers have immunity from prosecution for saying or doing things in the course of litigation while zealously advocating for their client. There is no attorney-client relationship between you and the opposing lawyer. So, they are only constrained by the attorney ethical rules.

Q: The complaint seeks $100 million in damages for a minor injury! Is that even legal?

A: Yes. It would be foolish, but it is legal. A plaintiff can claim as much in the prayer as they desire. There are no limitations when it comes to pleading damages.

Q: I was served at my office in front of co-workers! Is that an ethical violation?

A: No. The rules of civil procedure govern service of process. Office service is acceptable.

Q: What if I dodge service? Can I avoid liability that way?

A: No. Dodging service is dangerous. If attempts at home and office service fail, most states allow the attorney to "serve" you by publishing notice in the newspaper. If this occurs, you probably will not know it. Once reasonable publication occurs, you can be found in default by the court. Also, many states have "actual notice" provisions that assume service is accomplished if you learn you are being sued.

Q: What happens if I am defaulted?

A: The plaintiff will present a damages case against you to the judge outside of your presence. Most likely, the judge will award damages. Collection efforts will commence and your paychecks and bank accounts will be garnished. You will also likely lose any insurance coverage you might have once had.

Q: How long is a civil judgment good for?

A: Generally, ten years. But, they can be renewed and will follow you forever until satisfied. Attorney's fees and interest are also allowed in regard to collection efforts.

Q: How long do lawsuits take?

A: This varies by the court and jurisdiction. Most cases in a high court will take between one to three years. However, more-complex cases may take up to five or six years to resolve. Arbitrations are on a much shorter timeline than most trials.

Q: How often are civil cases tried to a jury?

A: Very rarely. The vast majority of cases are either settled or voluntarily dismissed by the plaintiff.

Q: How long are trials?

A: It varies depending upon the complexity, number of witnesses and court calendar. Your lawyer can answer this question for you better than I can. Typically, however, a short trial lasts between three to five days. A more complicated matter might take two to three weeks. Trials lasting three to four weeks are less common, but do occur regularly.

Q: I thought the insurance company was taking care of this. Do I even need to be involved?

A: Yes. All insurance contracts have clauses that require your cooperation in the event you are sued. If you do not cooperate, you risk losing your insurance coverage for the entire claim.

Q: I am not insured. Can I recover attorney's fees if I win?

A: Parties can only recover fees if allowed by statute or by contract. In most cases, the American system is not a "loser pays" situation. Each party is responsible for their own attorney fees.

Q: The amount of money plaintiff is demanding exceeds my insurance policy limits. What if I do not have enough?

A: You are responsible for any excess damages. You will receive a letter from your insurance company explaining this. Discuss the possibility of hiring a separate lawyer with the appointed insurance company counsel. In certain situations, you will want your own lawyer to demand a "limits settlement" to protect your personal assets from collection efforts. Discuss this with counsel.

Q: A lawyer was assigned to my case by my insurance company. Is he really my lawyer?

A: Yes. The assigned insurance defense lawyer has a dual representation relationship. He or she represents both you and the insurance company. That lawyer cannot act adversely to your interests under the ethical rules. However, because the lawyer also represents the insurance company, they cannot advise you about certain things, such as certain coverage issues under your insurance policy.

Q: What is a "reservation of rights?" I just received this type of notice in the mail.

A: It means that your insurance company is paying for your defense costs, but they are not agreeing to cover you for damages, settlement or an adverse jury verdict. This usually has something to do with the way the claim was plead against you. There is a question whether your conduct is excluded under the insurance policy. For instance, a bar fight might be excluded, but the plaintiff's lawyer made it sound like you were negligent in the complaint. Consult with your own independent lawyer about coverage issues.

Q: Will a settlement protect me from being sued again by the same plaintiff?

A: If drafted appropriately, once the case is settled and dismissed "with prejudice" you can never be sued by the plaintiff for the same thing again, even if they suffer future injuries or damages associated with the original claim.

Q: My attorney bills me by the hour. What does that mean?

A: Attorneys are not paid for a product or an outcome. We are paid for our brainpower. If we are thinking about strategy, formulating a plan, writing a letter, or talking on the phone, we are working on your case. Most attorneys bill in six-minute intervals. If we spend eight minutes, you are billed for twelve.

Q: How can I keep the attorney's fees down?

A: Keep communications short, infrequent, and purposeful. Do not chat it up with your lawyer. E-mails work wonders. If we are not talking to you, we are working on another case. Many lawyers bill clients for small talk because it is billable time lost on another case. The general rule of thumb is that if the lawyer brings up small talk, it is not billed. But, if clients talk my ear off on the phone when I am trying to get work done on other matters, they are billed.

Q: How often should I check on my case?

A: Talk to your lawyer about this. Some clients like to be more involved than others. Work out an arrangement that works for you. Lawyers are flexible.

Q: Should I talk to witnesses?

A: No. Give the names of witnesses to your lawyer. Any discussion you have will be unprotected and the subject of inquiry during your deposition.

Q: Can I talk to my spouse about the case?

A: Yes. Spousal communications are privileged.

Q: Once I file a lawsuit, is my physician-patient privilege waived?

A: Generally not.

Q: If I agree to settle my case, will my insurance be affected?

A: Possibly. You must speak directly with your insurance carrier about this because your lawyer is prohibited from getting into this with you. For that matter, they probably have no idea.

ABOUT THE AUTHOR

Troy S. Bundy is a partner and shareholder at Hart Wagner LLP, one of the largest trial law firms in the Pacific Northwest. He obtained his BA from the University of Colorado in 1991, where he majored in political science and criminology. Thereafter, he obtained his JD from Lewis & Clark, Northwestern School of Law in 1994. Mr. Bundy is currently licensed to practice in both Oregon and Washington, where he specializes in professional liability defense and catastrophic injury claims.

ASPATORE